GET A PHD IN YOU:

BUSINESS EDITION

MASTER
YOURSELF
TO
CRUSH IT
AT
WORK
(AND LIFE)

SPECIAL GUEST
**BONUS
CHAPTER**
• INSIDE •

JULIE REISLER
AUTHOR OF *GET A PHD IN YOU*

GET A PHD IN YOU: BUSINESS EDITION

Master Yourself to Crush It at Work (and Life)

Julie Reisler

Tradepaper ISBN: 978-0-692-16694-9
Digital ISBN: 978-0-692-16657-4

Cover: Dino Marino
Photo Credit: Danielle Visco and Ariel Lewis
Interior Design: Christina Gorchos

Endorsements

"You are meant to thrive, be successful and be your You-est You®. Julie shows you exactly how to maximize your strengths, leverage your skills, and choose a life of abundance. *Get a PhD in YOU: Business Edition* is the playbook to help you achieve inner and outer mastery and success. Make the choice and master your career and life!"

—David Osborn, *New York Times* Best Selling Author of *Wealth Can't Wait* and *Miracle Morning Millionaires*

"*Get a PhD in YOU: Business Edition* is a must-read for anyone who wants to take their career, business and personal life to the next level. This book is a brilliant guide and playbook to help you master your inner world in order to create your ideal outer world. Most of us already know that the most important aspects of being successful are creating habits, goals and new ways of thinking that will support your highest potential. This book will give you exactly that, and so much more. Julie shows you how to be your You-est You and leverage your strengths. If you are an entrepreneur, working on your career or wanting to monetize your purpose, *Get a PhD in YOU: Business Edition* is essential to your inner and outer success."

—Hal Elrod, #1 Bestselling Author, *The Miracle Morning* (MiracleMorningBook.com)

"We don't always think that knowing ourselves is the key to business success, but Julie has managed to not only show how important self-awareness can be but gives us a logical path to follow. *Get a PhD in YOU: Business Edition* is a field guild to discovering which parts of yourself you want to bring into the world more fully. This book is not only an amazing journey but what it challenges you to uncover will change how you run and grow your business for the better. This book is a must-have for all business owners who believe that what we create in this world is a reflection of who we are."

—Dana Malstaff, CEO of Boss Mom, LLC

"Julie is an absolute badass authentic leader who walks her walk and is eager to help you thrive. You will want to read, re-read, and share *Get a PhD in YOU: Business Edition* with as many people as possible, as Julie reveals incredible insights, strategies, and game-changing principles that will help you take your career, and life, to new heights. The wisdom in this book is priceless and there's no doubt after working through it, you'll master yourself and crush it in all areas of life!"

—Rob Dial, Speaker, Coach, Podcast Host

"Julie is an expert on how to operate at your best, build self-worth, and live your purpose. *Get A PhD in YOU: Business Edition* is a business book that accomplishes all of these things, and more. Julie knows self-awareness is key and leads to self-mastery. She has helped me and countless others learn this truth: the answers you seek come from within. This book is packed with wisdom, principles, and tools to help you tap into your highest strengths and thrive in business and in life. Julie will save you the trouble of coming to the end of your journey and saying, "is this it?" She's been there before."

—Jesse Harless, Founder of Entrepreneurs in Recovery, Coach, Speaker

SPECIAL INVITATION

M any individuals have gathered in an online community to share ideas, render support, and promote accountability. When I first wrote *Get a PhD in YOU: Business Edition*, I envisioned helping numerous employees, entrepreneurs and those wanting to up-level their career shatter the belief that it's hard to monetize your purpose. I had no idea what was in store, and the result is an amazing growing community of people like you who want to have purpose and meaning in their career, a deeper mastery of self, and enjoy success of all kinds.

I'd like to personally invite you to join the PhD in YOU Business Mastermind community at JulieReisler.com/MasterYourself and Facebook.com/groups/PhDinYOUBusiness where you will find motivation, daily support, and help with any aspect of the book and crushing it at work.

You can connect with me personally on LinkedIn @JulieReisler, Instagram @JulieReisler, or on Facebook.com/JulieReislerLifeDesigner. Thank you so much for your time. I look forward to connecting and hearing about how you are mastering yourself and crushing it in all areas of life!

Table of Contents

INTRODUCTION

"To know thyself is the beginning of wisdom."

~SOCRATES

Welcome! I'm truly excited to share this book with you. I have seen the benefits of this material creating massive positive changes in the workplace and on the ladder of success.

Here's a powerful statistic that will hopefully add motivation to working through this book. I recently read in a study that the chances of being born are an astonishing 1 in 14 trillion. There are 7 billion people in the world, and your chances of being here are one in two-thousandth the size of our total earth population. You probably wouldn't make a business decision based on those odds. You can't deny that these numbers point to your being here for a greater purpose. Think about it: you have unique skills and talents that only you possess, being the 1 in 14 trillion who was graced with life. Doesn't that make you want to create a life as fulfilling and full of growth, learning, and success as possible? I'd imagine that you are also looking to make a positive impact in your job, organization, and career, and, frankly, to crush it at work and in life.

I'm curious to know if you actively consider each day that your strengths are unique to you and that you, being among the 1 in 14 trillion chances of being here, have talents that are waiting to be fully expressed within your job? Maybe you do. Most of us don't. So, how are you showing up at work, in your career, and in your life? You are a whole person, and contrary to belief, you can't leave part of yourself at work and part of yourself at home. You take all of your strengths, growth opportunities and beliefs wherever you are. Are you allowing limiting beliefs to get in the way of finishing a project you care about? Are you letting self-doubt stop you from being a powerful leader? Are you focusing on your own natural strengths and those of your teammates?

"Employee engagement is the art and science of engaging people in authentic and recognized connections to strategy, roles, performance, organization, community, relationship, customers, development, energy, and happiness to leverage, sustain, and transform work into results."

—DAVID ZINGER, *Let's Co-Create an Employee Engagement Charter,* The Employee Engagement Network

We know that an astounding 87 percent of employees are disengaged at work and unaware of this fact (Gallup study). It's time to shift these statistics, to tap into our natural skills, curiosity, and innate desire to add value in whatever role you are in. Not surprisingly, those employees who are highly engaged outperform their colleagues by 147 percent in earnings per share (Gallup study).

By working through this powerful book of often-overlooked principles for business success, you are already ahead of the game. Whether you are a manager, director, supervisor, entrepreneur, intern, president or hourly worker, YOU are crucial to the inner workings and overall human system.

However, before you look at what is working or not working within the system, you must first focus on you. It's time to shine the spotlight on your habits, beliefs, and energies, in order to home in on how you're showing up on the field at work. Where are you working to capacity? Where might you have room for growth? What habits aren't serving you or your career? Every human has an opportunity to grow and develop. If you aren't sure about your need for growth, you might want to pause and look at your complacency with where you are. There is no judgment if you are complacent, just know that the effort, energy, and intention you put into your job is what you'll get back. Want more satisfaction, greater creative involvement or a higher salary? If so, I'd invite you to first look at your beliefs around personal development.

I can hear some of your grumbles right now. You might fear that I'm taking you into the land of soft touchy-feely ickiness. We'll address that later. For now, I'm asking you to put aside your judgment, open your mind and see what might be possible for you after working through this book. (As a side note, keeping an open mind will serve you in all areas, not just with moving up in your career.)

Let me explain why we're doing this work. You can't give to others what you don't have. It takes courage to understand that you are the common denominator in your life. It pays off to research and study your life motivations, interests, and dreams, just as you'd pursue a PhD. Except in this book, instead of researching other subjects, the subject is YOU.

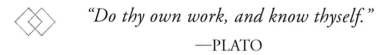 *"Do thy own work, and know thyself."*
—PLATO

In case you're curious, I do walk my talk. I have found that investing my own time, resources, energy, money, and emotions into learning more about me results in massive payoffs and exciting opportunities that continue to come into my career and life.

My first job taught me that I can't truly give of my talents or feel content until I have awareness of, and acceptance for, myself. This foundation of self-understanding is priceless. There is nothing money can buy that will provide you the inner calm and self-contentment gleaned from doing this work. You might hit some bumps in the road, or even get a flat tire, so to speak. That is to be expected. We'll look at how to handle such stressors and reframe them in a way that will truly serve you. Change comes out of sweat, work and, occasionally, pain. Just look at the metamorphosis process.

Going through rough patches with the new tools in this book will help you in ways you can't yet fathom, in both your career and your overall life.

What do I Mean by Getting a PhD in YOU in Business?

Getting a PhD in YOU in Business is about deeper self-awareness, mindset shifts, and creating effective change from within to bring about success in your career and life. It is about mastering your inner workings and habits to fully crush it at work.

In this book, you'll engage in a journey of mental shifts. These shifts are to be nurtured in the soil of self-learning.

You'll notice that nature is used as a primary teacher. So much of what we take for granted in nature leaves clues about how we can evolve, grow, learn and succeed. Take an acorn, for example. The acorn by itself is just unbridled potential. Plant it and give it the sun, water, nutrients, and time it needs, and soon enough you'll have a solid and sturdy oak tree.

All plants and trees crave—and typically need—sunlight to grow. Most trees, plants, and flowers are heliotropes, which means they grow toward the sun, along the way bending, moving, and ending up shaped in the direction of the sun. Like plants, we need light to grow. I invite you to see this book as a way to shed light on your opportunities to enhance your self-knowledge, strengths, and performance.

*"Awareness is like the sun.
When it shines on things, they are transformed."*
~THICH NHAT HANH

You'll start with honing your awareness, learning the importance of micro-steps, and paying attention to your body's biofeedback. You'll release the mental habits that no longer serve you as you create new narratives that inspire and propel you forward. By the completion of this journey, you will have more clarity about your strengths, your purpose, and your true capabilities. You'll see how purpose and inspiration show up in your career and day-to-day life. You'll choose your next steps forward. All of this sets the stage for you to live and experience a more inspired and empowered career and life.

The Three Main Modules

This book is divided into three main modules that should be fairly easy to remember: **P – H – D.**

The first module, **P**, is for **Past**, which encompasses Chapters One and Two and is about combing through your past life story to find your best and greatest strengths. You will look at what stale and limiting beliefs might be getting in the way of your performance, as well as when you've been at your peak state or have had your best experiences in your career and in life.

The second module—**H** for **Honor**, which you'll find in Chapters Three, Four, and Five—is all about honoring your strengths, skills, talents, unique attributes, and whole self, in and out of work.

The third and final module, **D**, is for **Direction** and is found in Chapters Six, Seven, and Eight. Without direction, work and life can be aimless and without a powerful purpose and "why." Getting clarity on what direction you want for your life is important for goal setting and knowing where you want to steer your ship.

The Get a PhD in YOU: Business Edition Game "Rules":

The game rules to help you be successful are very simple.

> **Rule #1:** Keep an open mind while playing full throttle.
>
> **Rule #2:** Self-judgment is out of bounds.
>
> **Rule #3:** Cultivate a "time out and tune-in" mindset.
>
> **Rule #4:** Keep the spotlight on the real focus: YOU.
>
> **Rule #5:** Respect the process and ditch your stopwatch.

Let's unpack these rules together. Following them will not only help you advance at a faster pace, but they will be great assets to incorporate in all parts of your life.

1. Keep an open mind while playing full throttle.

One of the most difficult things to change is human behavior. You certainly can't make a change with a fixed mindset, which is why one of the most important aspects in this course is keeping an open mind. It is a gift to give yourself and those around you. I'd encourage you to stay open to everything you read and learn about in this book. That doesn't mean you have to believe or accept it all. Do yourself a favor, though: be open, and if you notice that you are judging, complaining or mocking any of the material covered or questions asked, pause and perhaps tap your head to remind yourself to be open-minded (it always helps when you can add a physical link to a new habit). Watch what happens in your life as well, as you learn this powerful tool.

2. Self-judgment is out of bounds.

Activities that increase self-awareness often bring up feelings of insecurity, frustration, disappointment in self, and judgment. It's a normal human response, but not one that you need to keep around. Let's make a rule, shall we? Self-judgment is out of bounds and is not permitted in this game. You're going to need to be your own referee here. I can't blow a whistle every time I hear you go into self-judgment, but you can, in your mind. If you notice yourself going out of bounds with self-critique, you could point your finger and arm in front of you to signal, "I'm out of bounds."

3. Cultivate a "time-out and tune-in" mindset.

I remember learning deep in the experience of rearing two children under the age of three the concept of "time-out." There are many methods, but the one I used most often was coordinating the time-out in minutes corresponding to the number of years the child was. For example, when my daughter, Dalia, was three years old, I'd give her three minutes of time-out. Often, I used it when she seemed cranky, tired, or over-stimulated. This concept isn't likely new to anyone, but one of the best-kept secrets I learned over the years was realizing I could give myself a time-out. I'd also feel tired, cranky. and overwhelmed at times, so I'd lock myself in my room or bathroom for a few moments of peace and solace. You could adopt giving yourself a time-out in the number of minutes of your age as well. The point is, as you are experiencing new ideas and playing with different concepts, you might find yourself feeling a little overwhelmed, uneasy, or unsure. Part of what you'll be learning is to home in on your innate guidance system, so be sure to give yourself a time-out so you can tune in if needed. We'll get into this later, as intuition is one of the cornerstones to your innately powerful guidance system.

4. Keep the spotlight on the real focus: YOU.

What most of us do is to put the blame on someone else. We don't mean to, and often we do it subconsciously. In order to make something conscious and part of your competency, you have to first take it out of your blind spot. This is why I'm encouraging you to start being aware of how you're taking responsibility (or not) for your career and life. It's easy to focus on what others are doing or not doing, especially in the workplace. Language that will support you focusing on yourself involves words like "how" and "what" versus "why"

and "who." For example, if you become aware that your relationship with your colleague is not as stellar as you'd like, you might ask yourself, "What can I do to change this relationship?" versus "Why does she always act so insensitive to me?" This is true for any part of your life. Start taking responsibility for all your actions and, as I've heard it said before, stay in your own swimming lane. As you focus on yourself and change what you can, your outer world will soon reflect these positive shifts. Watch and note it for yourself. Keep a running tab of this list. You'll be amazed.

5. Respect the process and ditch your stopwatch.

If you're like me, you might run a bit on the impatient side. Many of us—especially in our Type A, fast-paced society—want to accomplish our goals and have success right now. With learning and changing habits, however, the "I must have it now" mentality will not work. Scientifically, we know that re-wiring and changing habits in your brain takes anywhere from 60 to 120 days (the average person taking 67 days). This is not an overnight process, and it's better to get yourself in a frame of mind now that acknowledges the small wins and the time it takes to create real change. My recommendation is to ditch your stopwatch and respect that this process is changing how you think, work, interact with others, and digest your work and life.

Why a Powerful Course in YOU?

You may be wondering why we're putting so much focus on you, and the reason is that you can't give what you don't have. In the workplace, this comes down to energy, time, resources, creativity, innovation, engagement, and profitability. In short, by investing in your own mindset, you are investing in your role in your job, team, organization, and even the economy.

There is only one of YOU in your office, job, company, family, community, and world. Each of us is born with distinct interests, powerful talents, and unique skills. I know your company, organization, or workplace will benefit tremendously from your willingness to uncover YOU so you can bring your best self to work and share your voice, purpose, and contribution from your own unique perspective. Most importantly, you will benefit from the changes in your entire life.

The Stages

As your guide and facilitator on this important adventure, I want to thank you for stepping up to the plate and choosing to invest in your self-awareness tool bag. The stages of growth will set you free! You can assume you'll go through the following stages as you move through this book:

Stage 1: Eagerness, as in, "I'm eager to see what this is all about."

Stage 2: Judgment, where you might find yourself wondering, "What the heck did I get myself into?"

Stage 3: Overwhelm, such as, "There is way more here than I thought."

Stage 4: Light-bulb Moments, where you start to realize: "This is powerful stuff."

Stage 5: Acknowledgement, a.k.a. being able to say, "I did it. I am seeing the results!"

As a coach, my aim is to create sustainable change and the opportunity for you to thrive at the individual level and as part of the human system. This book is your personal office space for growth. In a world of distraction, this book reminds you that your most important focuses are your choices, habits, and performance.

Know that your focused energy, along with your efforts, will help direct you. We all have layers of comparative thinking and socialized beliefs that dull our effectiveness and potential. This book is designed to help you strip away anything that tampers your excellence. Know that these stages are normal, to be expected, and part of the growth process.

Make This a Pivotal Starting Point

Less than a decade ago, I woke up in the middle of the night in a sheer panic, heart pounding, ceiling spinning, drenched in sweat, and unsure if I would be alive the next morning. My body was telling me that the way I was doing work and life was not working. I soon found out that I had an autoimmune condition called Hashimoto's (hypo-thyroiditis). It is a life-long condition that affects your thyroid, which oversees your metabolism and internal heating and cooling system. Many women tend to be affected by an overactive or underactive thyroid, and the blame is often given to the starring role of stress. There is no doubt that my whirlwind life of being overworked, overstressed, and overwhelmed had come to a crashing halt. In addition to working a full-time job as the Director of Recruiting and Director of Guest Relations for the most successful franchise of a Fortune 500 restaurant chain, I was simultaneously getting a master's degree, raising two children under the age of six, separating from my husband (although amicable, still quite stressful), pursuing a coaching certificate and personal training certification, and coaching in an intensive personal development program (I know, doing all at the same time was insanity). As an experiential student of life, I quickly learned the hard way. My body was on overload, and my energy was frazzled. While quite scary, this wake-up call resulted in my doing a major YOU-turn at work and in my life. As a result, I ended up shifting gears big time so I could heal, retrain myself how to do life in moderation and be successful with an improved mindset, a toolbox of new habits, and plenty of self-care.

My goal is for you to avoid the wake-up call and start managing your mind, energy and actions now, so you don't have to end up with a lifetime ticket to an autoimmune condition. While it has turned out to be a great teacher in my life, I certainly would not recommend it. We will look at how our mindset and physical body are connected and discover together that many of us are living in a personal energy emergency.

If you long to feel more than just competent and "fine" at your job or in life, start here. Society gives you generalized measurements for success. I'm giving you the tools to realize your true individual purpose and value. My purpose is to help you discover the seeds to your power and the creative genius that lies within you. They won't be found outside of you. You hold these keys.

The roadmap you need to succeed is implanted within.

As you progress through this self-guided study of YOU, it is my hope you will embrace this previously untraveled road. I believe you can achieve a *new* kind of PhD: a "Doctorate of Potential" for envisioning and creating the potential and outcomes you desire.

Here's to you crushing it!

Julie

Getting YOU Ready: Checklist & Mindset

 "Your attitude determines your altitude." ~Zig Ziglar

OK, before you dive into the deep end of the pool, make sure you've completed all of the checklist items. You wouldn't jump in without a bathing suit (well, maybe you would, but probably not on a business trip). Make sure you are suited up and ready to go.

◊ I have filled out the Workplace Well-Being Wheel

◊ I filled out the Personalized Energy Assessment

◊ I have a positive attitude and open mind

◊ I am ready for learning and change

◊ I am ready to take notes and be hands-on

◊ I have purchased/received a copy of *Get a PhD in YOU: Business Edition*

Additional Notes:

_____

_____

_____

_____

_____

_____

THE YOU CONTRACT

The YOU Contract is about setting an intention and committing to being your most successful self.

You can't make changes without a willingness to change. Before you engage in the most important learning of your lifetime—the study of YOU—I encourage you to sign this contract with, and for, yourself.

Make a copy and post it somewhere you will see it every day. Perhaps frame it and place it on your office wall or desk. You are embarking on a path of self-learning that will give you the keys to the kingdom of happiness, career success, accomplishment, and, most importantly, unleashed potential.

I, _____, am dedicated, eager and ready to uncover my strengths and interests, release unhelpful habits and stay open-minded to new experiences and beliefs. I agree to be present, persistent and poised to learn and change. When I am not feeling as focused or engaged, I will commit to staying in the game and actively participating in this book. I will not let one situation, experience, or limited thought get in my way. I will reframe the way I define "failure" as *my first attempt to learn*. I agree to the process of new awareness.

With each experience, I am open to learning, growing, and gaining new perspectives.

I am willing and ready to take on the study of me. I will be as serious and devoted to the study of me as I would be in any high-level project, graduate study, certification or work program. I will devote the necessary time, intention, attention, and curiosity needed. I am open to new insights so that I can call forth my talents and skills. I am here, I am committed to taking action, and I am game. I am willing to care for my mind, body and deeper connection to my purpose. I'm ready to bring it on and crush it at work!

_____   _____
Name   Date

Download a copy of The YOU contract to print, sign and hang up at:

JulieReisler.com/MasterYourself

Share it with others and encourage them to sign their own contract by posting it on social media with the hashtag #PHDINYOU.

MODULE ONE

PAST STORY

Chapter One

THE ROI OF INVESTING IN YOU

*"Your work is to discover your work and then with all
your heart to give yourself to it."*

-BUDDHA

There's no greater or more important study than the study of YOU.

You might ask why and want to challenge me on this. I hear you, and I'd encourage you to stay with me.

We become what we study. To have a successful career where you are growing, learning, thriving, and having a valuable impact, you have to know your strengths, growth opportunities, and blind spots. It is not enough to just be competent in your job. It is crucial that you are conscious.

Consciousness is bred out of awareness.

Awareness means you are awake, out of autopilot mode, and in the driver's seat of your life.

One of the keys to studying yourself is to take responsibility for every single action. This means not allowing yourself to get off the hook by shirking responsibility. You are hereby agreeing to be accountable for all aspects of your life.

"We do not act rightly because we have virtue or excellence,
but we rather have those because we have acted rightly.
We are what we repeatedly do. Excellence, then,
is not an act but a habit."

~ ARISTOTLE

In our current society, it's easy to see how popular it is to be a victim and blame someone else for your mishap. Our hypersensitivity to suing for any reason has created what I call "Victimerica." It's easy to be a victim and find fault with the other party. While warranted in a few cases, in many it's not. What's missing is our taking full responsibility for each and every action, decision, and choice. Therefore, we end up living life as victims. In victimhood, there is no room to look deeper at who you are and who you are not. You can sit back and point fingers at anyone and anything else. That is the land of *Victimerica*. Let's get off that land and voyage to "Responsamerica," where we all take responsibility for ourselves.

Studying yourself and taking responsibility is a courageous venture. While it is not for the faint of heart, it is actually more disheartening to live as a victim.

See for yourself. Look back at a time or moment when you might have blamed someone or something else for an issue you were part of. It could have been a project you were assigned to that wasn't successful. Perhaps you blamed the IT guy for not better explaining the new software or your HR director for not sharing the impact on employees. My guess is that you avoided the powerful question, "How could I have handled this project better?"

Depending on your chosen way to handle setbacks or "failure," you might have avoided looking bad.

Part of the reason we do this is because as human beings, we like to feel significant and look good. It's how we're wired. We crave connection, affirmation, and belonging. If you fear being frowned upon or not being liked, you might steer away from taking full responsibility.

Doing this work requires you to move through your fears so that you can grow, expand, and learn to your potential. The best learning experiences are not linear or without challenge. Repeat that one more time to yourself, and perhaps add it to a sticky note. *The best learning experiences are not linear or without challenge.* You'll want to keep this thought close at hand for moments that might be less than fun.

I believe that how we view ourselves affects how we view the others. Your inner realm determines your experience of your outer world. Understanding this is powerful. As you learn to master your inner world, you will master your outer world. We will dive into this later in the book.

Here's another key to remember: your mindset, thoughts, and actions are contagious. Think of a scenario where one of the people in a meeting was negative. What happened? I bet the entire room felt negative. You didn't see a flashing sign saying, "Josh is negative," but my guess is that you sensed it. Each of us is contagious when it comes to our emotions, whether we like it or not.

You are the common denominator of all your thoughts and experiences, as well as the steward of your mind. Not only does being a victim not serve you, it will hold you back. Conversely, realizing that you are the quarterback of your game (i.e. your job) will give you a whole new vantage point about responsibility.

In my own life, I had a massive mind shift when I stopped blaming others for a role I didn't want to do. The epiphany was mighty. I realized I was the one in charge of my actions, words, and decisions. I chose to look at my part in disliking my job, and in that analysis realized it was time to move on from my career of eleven years.

Gratitude

Instead of leaving my corporate job with frustration or blame, I left with gratitude and a deeper understanding of my strengths, growth opportunities, interests, and purpose. The power of gratitude is real, and there is scientific research on how it positively transforms our outlook, mind, and well-being. Studies show that when you start expressing gratitude more often, you lower your stress response, sleep better, experience less depression, improve your immunity, increase resilience, and feel more hopeful. (Amy Morin, "7 Scientifically Proven Benefits Of Gratitude That Will Motivate You To Give Thanks Year-Round," Forbes, November 23, 2014.)

Just like the air we breathe, gratitude is free and readily available. While there were many things about my former corporate job that I felt I had outgrown and didn't want to do, I can tell you that my gratitude for my experience far outweighs any past frustrations.

It's time to do a little pre-work to get in the best mental state possible. Each chapter builds upon the next, so take your time with this work and remember, there are no right or wrong answers.

5 Get a PhD in YOU:
Business Edition Questions Check-in

Why are you here?

What does your ideal career/job look like? Are you in that role now? If not, how might you get there?

_____

_____

_____

What would you attempt if you knew you could achieve success?

_____

_____

_____

Where am I now?

Describe your job right now (role, experience, full-time/part-time, ideal/not ideal).

_____

_____

_____

List the accomplishments you are most proud of at work or in your past career experience:

_____

_____

_____

What's working?

What are you naturally skilled at?

_____

_____

_____

What are your strengths?

_____

_____

_____

What do you enjoy doing?

_____

_____

_____

Where are you succeeding in your job?

_____

_____

_____

What's not working?

Where do you feel you're falling short?

_____

_____

_____

What are your biggest time wasters?

_____

_____

_____

What can you let go of/delegate?

_____

_____

_____

How can you move forward?

What is your ideal career future like?

_____

_____

_____

What do you want more of?

_____

_____

_____

What is your level of commitment (in a range of 1 – 10, with 1 being low and 10 being very high) to implementing new behaviors and creating change?

_____

_____

_____

GET AHEAD: GOALS & PURPOSE FOR SUCCESS

Goal-Setting Steps:

1. Imagine that today is your birthday, and as you blow out the candles, you can wish for anything you want to happen this year in your career. Take twenty minutes to brainstorm the top accomplishments you'd like to achieve this year in your job.

2. Comb through your list and circle your top three.

1. _____

2. _____

3. _____

4. _____

5. _____

6. _____

7. _____

8. _____

9. _____

10. _____

11. _____

12. _____

13. _____

14. _____

15. _____

16. _____

17. _____

18. _____

19. _____

20. _____

3. What would it take for you to accomplish these things? Who do you have to be in order to make this happen? For example, what are the character traits, beliefs, virtues, and mindset needed to be successful? Go back to the top three you circled and write down notes about these traits.

DAILY PROGRESS SHEET

Reminder: what you focus on expands.
Start tracking your progress and noting the small (and big) wins.

My light-bulb moments:

_____

_____

_____

My blind spots:

_____

_____

_____

My new habit to try:

_____

_____

_____

I will stay accountable by: _____

_____

_____

Accountability Winning Team

Professional athletes and performers have coaches and a support team. If it works for the pros, it will work for you. Create your accountability winning team to help you rewire your brain for greater success. Here are the guidelines and recommendations in forming your team.

1. Choose one to three trusted, positive people (colleagues, friends, or mentors).

2. Ask them to be on your team (and perhaps offer to be on their team).

3. Explain you are working through a new book, *Get a PhD in YOU: Business Edition*, and would be grateful to have an accountability partner/team.

4. You will check in with them daily (via text, email or voicemail message, if not in person or on the phone).

5. Daily check-ins will consist of:

    1. Light-bulb moments or new awareness

    2. An action you committed to taking that day, correlating to a new habit you are forming

    3. Three things you're grateful for

Pledge to Yourself

Make a decision to boldly study you—your inner dialogue, hidden beliefs, and limiting thoughts, along with everything that makes you tick. Decide to learn from all you encounter and let go of attachment to how that might look. Yes, sometimes this path is hard and at times very uncomfortable. If you've ever trained for a marathon or signed up to do something else outside of your comfort zone—such as public speaking when you dislike speaking on stages—you know that the experience will require you to extend your limits. Sometimes these moments aren't enjoyable. Choose instead to be present for the new discoveries in order to become more resilient, flexible, and adaptable. Know that as you are pushing your edges, you are growing. We are meant to learn and adapt. Take the moments when you see something you don't like about yourself as reminders that you are here to learn. Download the 5 business questions, check-in and pledge to yourself to make this a daily practice and continue your learning at juliereisler.com/masteryourself.

 "Be grateful for awareness of your blind spots, for without them there wouldn't be growth. Growth emerges and leads to a renewed motivation to soar higher than ever imagined."
-JULIE REISLER

Homework: Chapter 1

Accountability & Team Check-in Reminder

Daily Review:

1. Light-bulb moments or new awareness

2. An action you committed to taking that day, correlating to a new habit you are forming

3. Three things you're grateful for

Self-Reflection Journal Space

This is your journal space to use on a daily basis. Use it to reflect on your feelings and insights related to the chapter topic you have just covered.

Related to this chapter, think about the following: What have I learned about the importance of investing in myself? Why? What changes am I committed to working on throughout this course? What will I do to keep myself committed on a regular basis? What time can I dedicate to myself (daily, weekly)? What other nuggets of wisdom am I now seeing for myself?

Chapter Two

DO R&D ON YOURSELF

"Throw yourself into some work you believe in with all your heart;
live for it, die for it, and you will find happiness that you
had thought could never be yours."

~DALE CARNEGIE

Research and Reflection

Any successful company will do research and development before launching a campaign, product, or service. Profitability is connected to how you compare to the market; how does your product relate to another similar product? How are you going to differentiate yourself? How will you offer a service that is better than any other competing service? We accept that this is the process of creating a successful entity. The more you know how your product works or the detailed features it encompasses, the better you can share with and sell your product to the public. We wouldn't think of missing this step in business, yet we so often miss this step with ourselves. Let's not forget this sage advice:

"The only way to do great work is to love what you do."
~STEVE JOBS

Start Your Research and Development Now

You'll want to be like a scientist. Scientists are, in essence, trained to do research and development (R&D). In order to come up with findings to a hypothesis, they have to first do their research. Which means that change starts with research and also requires patience, practice, pace, and persistence.

A great place to start is by doing a cost-benefit analysis of YOU. The aim is to look at your strengths and natural talents and note where you are using or not using them in your current position. What you appreciate, appreciates.

The Solution is Appreciative Inquiry

I partnered with Jon Berghoff, creator of the LEAF Appreciative Inquiry Certification and President of FLI, the leading provider of Appreciative Inquiry Summits globally. Having worked with Jon while I earned my LEAF Certification, he agreed to create a custom chapter at the end of the book (see chapter nine) to take every lesson you learn to whole new levels of impact. I had studied the power of Appreciative Inquiry in my master's degree program in coaching, and can tell you that learning to use this framework with both individuals and larger systems, is a game-changer.

Appreciative Inquiry (AI), developed by David Cooperrider in the 1970's, is at its core the search for the absolute best in a person, organization or system. As human beings, we often focus first on the negative. With an AI approach, you learn to change your lens and recognize what's working well, investigate why it's working, and find ways to do more of that. The basis of AI is that what we focus on and give attention to will expand and grow. This book is steeped in AI and uses an Appreciative Inquiry perspective to help you see the opportunities and possibilities available when you are working and living from your strengths. The goal is to ask new appreciative-based questions that allow you to see your—and the system's—talents, skills, strengths, opportunities, and wins.[1]

A human system works most efficiently, effectively, and successfully when strengths are derived from each individual. In order to bring the best out of

any company, group, or team, it is helpful to know your strengths. Having a diverse set of strengths and talents to draw upon is what makes the most impactful growth, change, and development of any team, company, or culture.

"I consider my ability to arouse enthusiasm among men the greatest asset I possess. The way to develop the best that is in a man is by appreciation and encouragement."
– CHARLES SCHWAB

Let's dive deeper into your past to review where you thrive and feel most in sync with your skills, talents, and interest, and where you might be getting stuck.

Career Strengths Inquiry: these questions are designed to uncover and highlight your best experiences or achievements from your past career history.

1. When in the past (in your current position or in another job) have you felt most successful, thriving, or in alignment with or connected to your strengths?

_____

_____

_____

---

1   AI definition and ideas from: Stavros, Jacqueline, Godwin, Lindsey, & Cooperrider, David, "Appreciative Inquiry: Organization Development and the Strengths Revolution," *Practicing Organization Development: Leading Transformation and Change*, Edition: Fourth, Chapter 6 [New Jersey: John Wiley & Sons, Inc., 2016], 96-116.

_____

_____

2. What were you doing? Try to remember as many details as you can about the experience, situation, or encounter, and jot them down. Feel free to write as many as come to mind.

_____

_____

_____

_____

3. How did you feel? What made this such a memorable experience?

_____

_____

_____

_____

4. List what you perceive to be your greatest strengths (examples: You are logical, creative, resilient, emotionally intelligent, determined, problem solver, visionary, motivated, goal oriented, etc.).

_____

_____

_____

_____

_____

5. Now turn your attention to a moment, experience, or time in your past career where you felt like you weren't using or aligned with your greatest strengths or skills. List one to three examples of what you were doing.

_____

_____

_____

_____

6. How did it feel in these instances not to be using your greatest strengths? What can you learn from this experience? What are you ready to eliminate?

_____

_____

_____

_____

If you're feeling inspired to see where your strengths carry over into other aspects of your life, fill out the following strengths inquiry for your personal life.

Personal Strengths Inquiry: these questions are designed to uncover and highlight your best experiences or moments from your past personal history.

1. When have you felt your best, and most in alignment with, or connected to, your strengths, talents, skills, or gifts?

_____

_____

_____

_____

2. What were you doing? Try to remember as many details as you can about the experience, situation, or encounter, and jot them down. Feel free to write as many as come to mind.

_____

_____

_____

_____

3. How did you feel? What made this such a memorable experience? Write as many feelings as you can remember.

_____

_____

_____

_____

4. List what you perceive to be your greatest strengths in life (examples: You are compassionate, open-minded, creative, resilient, determined, a problem solver, kind, emotionally intelligent, motivated, goal oriented, etc.).

_____

_____

_____

_____

5. Now turn your attention to a moment, experience, or time in your past where you felt like you weren't using or aligned with your greatest strengths and skills. List one example of what you were doing and experiencing.

_____

_____

_____

_____

6. How did it feel in these instances not to be using your greatest strengths? What can you learn from this experience? What are you ready to let go of?

_____

_____

_____

_____

Combing through your data from both inquiries, what are you now noticing about yourself? Is there anything that is a surprise to you? Are you using these strengths in your career and your personal life? If not, how might you start infusing your strengths into your career and/or personal life?

> Empirical meta-analysis of the human side of enterprise—of employee well-being, happiness, and engagement—has demonstrated that productivity, profits, employee retention, and customer obsession all increase as the level of workplace well-being, particularly employee personal growth, increases.[2]

Take a moment to journal below about your new awareness and "a-ha's."

"The most crucial relationship is the one you have with yourself. Focus on building a rock-solid relationship with you first, then create and nurture all other relationships from there."

~JULIE REISLER

---

[2] David Cooperrider, "Mirror Flourishing: The New Business North Star," *Kosmos Journal for Global Transformation*, Spring/Summer 2016.

Homework: Chapter 2

Accountability & Team Check-in Reminder

Daily Review:

1. Light-bulb moments or new awareness

2. An action you committed to taking that day, correlating to a new habit you are forming

3. Three things you're grateful for

Self-Reflection Journal Space

This chapter emphasized the power of doing research on yourself and uncovering your strengths. Use this chapter's journaling pages to capture your findings of what brings out your best.

Writing prompt: If you want some help focusing on what you learned in this chapter, you can use the following writing prompts to begin your journaling.

- In order to be my best, I need to...

- Ways I will utilize my strengths in my career are...

- Ways I will utilize my strengths in my personal life are...

MODULE TWO:

HONOR

Chapter Three

TO BE OR NOT:

THE POWER OF BEING

*"You must master a new way to think before you
can master a new way to be."*

~MARIANNE WILLIAMSON

We often underestimate the power of our non-verbal communication. According to Professor Emeritus of Psychology Albert Mehrabian, approximately 93 percent of communication is not based on your words, yet has everything to do with your tone, body language, eye contact (or lack thereof), and thoughts and feelings about yourself and whomever you are communicating with. I'd make the case that how you are being, meaning how you see yourself in the world and internally at that moment, has everything to do with how you communicate and translate your message.

Most of your ability to influence and successfully communicate has to do with everything other than what you're actually saying. If more companies understood this, they would focus intently on training employees all of the non-verbal aspects of effective communication. You should applaud your organization and yourself for understanding this to be a key component to cultivating a successful team and business.

In essence, *you* don't decide if you are a good communicator; everyone else makes that call. Much of your communication results from your internal drive, confidence, commitment, integrity, viewpoint, self-worth, perspective, and beliefs.

As human beings, we are programmed to naturally pick up on non-verbal cues such as a frown, smile, smirk, or other facial movements. Your bodily movements, gestures, and postures are subconscious. They happen without thought or planning and are directly related to what you believe to be true. Therefore, if you are leading a team meeting trying to build trust and partnership, yet you don't believe you can trust your colleagues, your words will say one thing and your body language will say another. When this inconsistency happens, we interpret the person communicating with us to be untrustworthy or in some way not believable.

This is why the internal work you do to create a state of being that is based on trust, confidence, self-worth, possibility, and success is crucial. Without making this internal shift within yourself, you will be less successful in proactively communicating, motivating, and empowering yourself and your colleagues.

To answer the question, "to be or not to be," understand first that we are always "being" or committed to something. Remember, we are called human *beings* for a reason.

Being Awareness Activity One:

1. What is your internal way of being? (For example, optimistic, trustful, distrustful, competitive, open-minded, aggressive, arrogant, humble, compassionate, lacking empathy, etc.)

_____

_____

_____

_____

2. What do you believe about your talents? What are your natural skills? Do you believe you have the skills, smarts and motivation needed to be successful in your current role?

_____

_____

_____

_____

3. What do you believe about yourself in relation to the others you work with?

_____

_____

_____

_____

This activity allows you to get a deeper understanding of your inner beliefs about yourself and thus how others experience you. Our inner world determines our outer world.

Being Awareness Activity Two:

1. Look back at your career and jot down three positive situations where your actions were in alignment with your beliefs, which then lead to a successful outcome:

    a._____

    b._____

    c._____

2. What were your internal beliefs about yourself, the project and your team? How were you being in those situations? (For example: "I was being open and trusting of myself and others," "I was being compassionate, open-minded and committed to excellence," etc.)

    a._____

    b._____

    c._____

3. Can you see a link to how success grew out of how you were being? Reflect on this awareness.

_____

_____

_____

_____

Being Awareness Activity Three:

The best way to change your state of being is to decide and declare the value and mindset commitment you desire. What I mean by this is to create a positive statement (privately, maybe written in your journal, or publicly with your accountability partner) that declares what you are committed to. For example, "I am committed to being open-minded and empathetic in all my dealings with colleagues and myself. Because in doing so, I will expand my growth, learning, and ability to succeed, as well as impact my company."

Now you try it.

I am committed to being:_____

_____

_____

Because in doing so, I will: _____

_____

_____

We will further unpack the concept of linking your way of being to your energy later in Chapter Seven: "Harnessing Your Energy 101." The best way to keep learning is to take notice of the principles in this chapter about internal beliefs and ways of being and watch what unfolds in your life. The proof will show up in many forms—be it in a team meeting, group project, or performance evaluation.

One of the best ways to build your self-awareness muscle and learn how to be the kind of leader you'd want to work with is to develop a strong relationship with yourself. A great place to develop this 1:1 connection with yourself is while looking in the mirror. The more you learn to honor and connect with yourself, the more you will get honor and connection in return from your colleagues.

Want to know the state of how you experience yourself? Go to the bathroom in your office (preferably when no one is around) and look in the mirror. Stare into your eyes and listen to what you say to yourself. Is it: "I'm doing a stellar job today" (confidence) or perhaps you're saying, "I suck at this and feel like an imposter" (insecurity) or "I am better than they know and should have gotten that raise" (frustration & disappointment)? Download these powerful questions at juliereisler.com/masteryourself.

Try it. Then take note of the following.

What was your first reaction as you stared at yourself?

_____

_____

_____

_____

What voice (or thought) did you hear in reaction to that statement?

_____

_____

_____

_____

Do you feel differently about yourself now that you've done this? How?

_____

_____

_____

_____

Daily Powerful Practices #1: Mirror Management

How you view yourself is going to be how others view you. Remember, as human beings we communicate mainly through non-verbal means. If you are feeling insecure after being passed over for a promotion, lacking confidence in a new role, or feeling incompetent after being told you need to have better emotional intelligence, you will carry this feeling with you in how you see and view yourself. As social animals, we tune into other's thoughts, feelings, and energy. I'm sure you can recall a time when you were in a meeting and the energy felt awful because of one person who was in a terrible mood. Remember, we are contagious. Learning to harness your energy, manage your emotions, and feel confident will pay enormous dividends.

Mirror Management means being able to connect with yourself fully—including your purpose, drive, passions, and worthiness. It will drive your confidence up and give you greater access to how you can add more value to your career and your life. While I teach this as a basic life skill and habit, it is equally as powerful in the workplace. All you need is a mirror nearby: in your car, at your work restroom, or at home as you're dressing for an important meeting. We know from speakers such as Amy Cuddy in her "Your Body Language May Shape Who You Are" TED talk that actions like standing in a power pose can alter the way you perform in an interview or at a meeting. Mirror Management will help you to connect on a deeper level to yourself and to others.

Managing Mirror Management

What you say to yourself impacts how you feel and what you believe. This practice allows you to pay attention to the words you choose and how those words make you feel. Want to change how you talk to yourself or others? Try at least one of these Mirror Management phrases every day. Pick and choose the one that resonates with you, or make up your own. It is important that you feel the statement you are saying to yourself is true. Lying to yourself never works. If it doesn't feel accurate or applicable, then don't use it and find another one that does feel right for you.

Mirror Management Statements:

Self-connection

- I am committed to excellence.

- I am open to seeing my talents and blind spots.

- I have important skills and talents to share.

- Failure is part of the growth process.

- I appreciate all setbacks as growth opportunities.

- I choose to grow and learn every day.

- I have everything I need to be successful.

- I am learning every day.

- I forgive myself for all my past mistakes.

- I trust myself and my decisions.

- My ideal job is related to my willingness to learn.

- Today, I am full of energy and purpose.

- I share my knowledge freely with colleagues.

- I am learning to take better care of my well-being.

- I am learning how to tolerate differing opinions.

- I appreciate the job I'm in right now.

- The three things I am grateful for right now are...

Download these Mirror Management Statements to hang up on your own mirror at **juliereisler.com/masteryourself**

Your turn. Take a stab at it. Try writing your own Mirror Management phrases below.

_____

_____

_____

_____

Make Mirror Management a Daily Habit

Saying the phrase "I am here to share my purpose" or looking at yourself in the mirror and repeating "I really want to grow and take good care of you" has enormous benefits. By doing **Mirror Management** *every day*, you are creating your mindset to be one of positive self-belief. This belief about yourself was not formed overnight, and it will not shift overnight. Change in habit of thought takes time. Be patient and persistent during this process.

Start practicing by saying encouraging phrases to yourself using any mirror you come across. Remember, your colleagues can't hear your inner monologue. This is another free, easy, and potent tool to start incorporating now, particularly when you experience setbacks or challenges.

Had a rough conversation with your boss? Use your Mirror Management strategies to remind yourself that you are learning and growing, and this is part of the process. Feeling like your thoughts were not taken seriously in a meeting? Go to the restroom and remind yourself that your opinions are valuable and that you're learning to see things from a new perspective.

Success doesn't mean existing in a vacuum, free from critique, disagreement, and frustration. I'd argue that success is learning how to navigate the often choppy waters of life while remaining calm and collected in your own boat.

The Magic of Mirror Neurons

In neuroscience, there is an actual mirror neuron structure where specific parts of the brain become illuminated when observing an emotional experience outside of ourselves. For example, if you're playing a video game, you might actually feel like you're in the video game. The movie *Jumanji: Welcome to the Jungle* took this idea a little farther, but it's a similar concept.

We are able to create empathy through this mirror neuron system. As you can imagine, the study of this natural phenomenon is changing how we see and understand both empathy and the sharing and spreading of emotions amongst individuals and larger systems. How about the ability to cultivate empathy for yourself? Based on the mirror neuron principle, if you are able to cultivate empathy for yourself, others will then share an experience of empathy toward you. David Cooperrider discusses this idea in greater detail in the concept he has studied, which he calls "mirror flourishing." Cooperrider defines mirror flourishing as "the concrescence flourishing or growing together that happens naturally and reciprocally to us when we actively engage or witness in the acts that help nature flourish, others flourish, or the world as a whole to flourish. Mirror flourishing suggests an intimacy of relations between entities to the point where we can posit that there is no outside and inside, only the creative unfolding of an entire field of relations or connections."[3]

As you create a more powerful relationship with yourself, you are inadvertently positively affecting and encouraging your peers to do the same through mirror neurons. Imagine if your team or whole organization could feed off of one another seeking the best within oneself and with others.

Managing the mirror and changing the way you view yourself will show up positively in your conversations, projects, and bank account.

---

[3] David Cooperrider, "Mirror Flourishing: The New Business North Star," *Kosmos Journal for Global Transformation*, Spring/Summer 2016.

"Your inner beliefs will reflect your outer experiences.
Focus on being the kind of human being
you would most want to work with."

~JULIE REISLER

Homework: Chapter 3

Accountability & Team Check-in Reminder

Daily Review:

1. Light-bulb moments or new awareness

2. An action you committed to taking that day, correlating to a new habit you are forming

3. Three things you're grateful for

Self-Reflection Journal Space

This chapter emphasized the power of being and of words, both spoken aloud and internally to yourself as inner dialogue. Journal here what you have learned about the power of being. How does attitude affect your ability to fulfill your career goals?

Writing prompt: If you want some help focusing on what you learned in this chapter, you can use this writing prompt section to begin your journaling.

- I am beginning to take charge of creating the career I want by...

- What I learned about how I'm being is...

_____

_____

_____

_____

Chapter Four

MICRO-STEPS LEAD TO MACRO-LEAPS

"The journey of a thousand miles begins with a single step."

~LAO TZU

I'm not sure about you, but I've often been all about hitting the big goal, landing my dream client or accomplishing the big project (such as writing a book). As a recovering impatient entrepreneur, doing anything in small steps used to seem painful and frustrating. What I've learned in starting my own business, writing a book and accomplishing any tough project is that it's actually the small micro-steps that are worth being noted and celebrated, as they lead to the macro-leaps. What does that look like in our fast-paced, high-tech, and web-based world that focuses on before and after shots and big changes? It means redefining your expectations as well as your accomplishments on your terms.

Getting back to accessing wisdom from nature, look at how a tree releases its leaves in the fall, focuses energy inward in the winter, sprouts buds in the spring, and grows new leaves in the summer. That growth doesn't happen overnight. Neither does ours.

Practice Those Micro-Steps

We naturally grow and evolve behaviors over time. There are numerous studies around how our brains work that support the understanding that new thought patterns and habits take time, practice, and repetition. When we practice new thoughts or behaviors, our brain neurons literally start hanging out together and create whole new pathways that lead to the changes we desire. If you start to embrace all movements forward, even when it appears like you're going backward, you'll develop your muscles of self-confidence, resilience, grit, and perseverance. This will reinforce your desire to practice your new behavior more.

Trust me, I understand wanting the big win now. Let this be an intensive micro-step boot camp; I invite you to join me. It's a shift in perspective. It means going against what most companies focus on: the end result. Let's try an exercise to get a sense of how you might apply this to your career.

Grab a pen or your laptop and let's see what opens up here!

1. Look at a big win in your career and write it down. If you're feeling adventurous, write two or three. (*For example, I left my stable and cushy job to start my own business.*)

_____

_____

_____

_____

2. When you analyze how this big change or goal was met, can you break down the time frame? (*For me, the first thing I did when I thought of leaving my job was identify my purpose, then I imagined how I'd coach clients...then I thought about who might be interested in coaching...and then I started to think of what kinds of clients I'd want to coach...until finally I chose a name, registered for a website and began from the bottom up creating my business.*) List the steps YOU took here.

_____

_____

_____

_____

When you are planting flowers, you get the soil ready, plant your seeds, and then water and nurture it a little most days. You don't yank up the seeds to see if they are growing. That would inhibit the growth process. Over the course of time, with more care, attention, and action, your seeds sprout and then bloom to become a bold array of flowers. These changes happen sometimes more slowly than imagined or hoped for. We don't always know what the seed-to-flower timeline is, yet it's clear that it happened one micro-step at a time.

Awareness point: The ego's job is to keep you safe, so the ego sees any change as scary and risky.

Self-sabotage and negative thinking are typical during transitions as your mind adjusts. You have to override ego-mind tendencies as you aim for personal growth. The baby steps help to make this manageable. One of my favorite thought leaders of all time, Oprah Winfrey, says this beautifully: "The key to realizing a dream is to focus not on success but significance—and then even the small steps and little victories along your path will take on greater meaning."

_____

_____

_____

_____

Recommitting to and focusing on your new thoughts and behavior could feel odd, even disingenuous, at first. This is a natural part of reprogramming your thoughts to better serve you. The new action is imperative for a shift to happen. We can't get new results if we stay stuck in the same old habits and behaviors. Once you commit to getting unstuck or creating a transformation, just know that micro-steps will pay off big time. Most world-class and inspirational leaders will tell you that it is the small, incremental habits and daily actions that lead to greatness and big wins. Arianna Huffington, author and co-founder of the _Huffington Post_ and Thrive Global, says it brilliantly: "But you have to do what you dream of doing even while you're afraid."

Here are more questions to ask yourself:

Where can you see an area in your job that would benefit from micro-steps?

_____

_____

_____

_____

What could those micro-steps be?

_____

_____

_____

_____

How might you appreciate or even celebrate the micro-steps?

_____

_____

_____

_____

Whom can you share your micro-step wins with?

_____

_____

_____

_____

Download these micro-step questions to continue your practice
of taking micro-steps to macro-leaps at
juliereisler.com/masteryourself

I encourage you to create a mindset and space for yourself where you are encouraged to focus on the micro-steps. Whether you are focusing on a work goal to hit your numbers or a health goal to lose twenty pounds, it will serve you to build a new appreciation for the micro-steps. Then when you do hit your macro-leap, you'll be that more excited, grateful and present.

"Focusing on the micro-steps is your golden ticket to crushing it and actualizing your macro-leap."

–JULIE REISLER

Homework: Chapter 4

Accountability & Team Check-in Reminder

Daily Review:

1. Light-bulb moments or new awareness

2. An action you committed to taking that day, correlating to a new habit you are forming

3. Three things you're grateful for

Self-Reflection Journal Space

Journal about the most important micro-steps you took this week in your career and/or life, and where you envision them leading. Review what area in your life would most benefit from these micro-steps. Consider what those micro-steps might be.

Writing prompt: If you want some help focusing on what you learned in this chapter, you can use this writing prompt to begin.

- I will acknowledge my micro-steps by ...

_____

_____

_____

_____

Chapter Five

THE SURPRISING POWER OF YOUR WORDS

"Your conversations help create your world. Speak of delight, not dissatisfaction. Speak of hope, not despair. Let your words bind up wounds; not cause them."

~TAO TE CHING

Here's the thing: we speak words all the time, and most of them don't support you being your best or building a successful career.

*"**I AM,** two of the most powerful words, for what you put after them shapes your reality."*

~ AUTHOR UNKNOWN

Do you believe that I AM are the two most powerful words you can utter? Don't just take my word for it; test it out for yourself. Let's try it now. Fill in the blanks below and gather the data for yourself.

After each "I am" statement, I want you to take a moment to pause, reflect and notice how that word made you feel. On a scale of 1–10 (1 being depleted and resigned, 10 being fully empowered and self-expressed), rate how you processed each statement from a physiological standpoint, meaning how you feel versus how you think. I ask you to check in this way because our emotions are quite accurate in guiding us to know how we are interpreting a situation.

1. Choose empowering words that feel true (example: hardworking, resourceful, conscientious, loyal, dedicated, confident, smart, capable, resilient, creative).

I am.... _____

I am.... _____

I am.... _____

I am.... _____

I am.... _____

2. Now choose disempowering words that you might resonate with (example: insecure, an imposter, not smart, disliked, fearful, stressed).

I am.... _____

I am.... _____

I am.... _____

I am.... _____

I am.... _____

Now, grab a pen and write down your notes. What did you notice with this exercise? How did it feel to say the empowering versus disempowering words? If you didn't notice any change or shift in your physiology or mental state, that is perfectly OK. You might consider trying this again at another time and/or starting to notice how you feel when you use certain words over others.

Your Word Creates Your World

I learned the phrase "your word creates your world," from Neil Roseman, a highly trained business leader and now friend. I met Neil while coaching with him in a personal development leadership program. He used these words often to explain his entire philosophy of life. The first time I heard him say this, a light bulb went off in my head. What if this were really true? I began to test it out and saw for myself that our words are generative. They evoke, develop, and bring forth our reality. We always have the power to choose our words and our reality. I like to imagine that our words (and thoughts) have fuel—they fuel what we say into existence.

"Allow your words to fuel your vision "
~JULIE REISLER

Word Creating World Activity

Recall a time when you said something to yourself that had a noticeable effect, either positive or negative, on your own life and perhaps with a colleague, team or group:

_____

_____

_____

_____

Be a Word Investigator

We are responsible for all of our relationships—be it at work or home—and how they unfold. I'm not saying that you deserve to be yelled at by your boss. I would encourage you, though, to see where you agreed to be in that role in order to learn and grow. These kinds of victim-aggressor relationships can be an indicator that a person has limiting thoughts about his or her own value and worthiness, or they are not being accountable for their part in the equation. We have probably all struggled with playing the victim in one form or another at various moments of our lives. The point is to recognize it, ask new questions of yourself and course correct.

Let's do some more digging here. There are some key points that I believe will make all the difference in your career, how you interact with your colleagues, your overall job satisfaction and your success in your role. One of the quickest ways to assess if you're in victim mode is to note how you feel about and talk to yourself. You can do this by keeping a running tab tracking what you say to yourself.

For example, go from being the victim to being accountable, such as:

Victim: "Why am I always the one who ends up getting the extra projects and work to do?"

Accountable: "How can I learn to see getting more work as an opportunity to grow? What are the gifts in having extra projects?"

I, too, have struggled with this. At one time, I was in a role that felt stifling and frustrating, and which was not fully using my talents. I started to notice how negative I sounded every time I would insert a complaint or share how distraught I was. I started to see that my energy was depleted; I felt tired, overwhelmed, unhappy and annoyed. Since my actions clearly didn't reflect any willingness to change jobs, I saw that something else had to change. I decided to change the words I was saying to myself and made a conscious effort every day to look for growth opportunities and gifts from my job. Incredibly, after only a few days, I started to see my job through a different lens.

Let's dig a little deeper into words that support you and give you energy versus words that take away your power and put you in a negative state.

Word Inquiry:

1. What low-energy or disempowering word or phrase do you use too often?

_____

_____

_____

_____

2. What is a favorite high-energy or empowering word or phrase?

_____

_____

_____

_____

No matter what career or life situation you have created or are encountering, you always have the option to choose your words and language to support your best self. It is not always easy, especially when you feel victimized or entitled to something different.

Here's an activity to start playing with this concept.

Choosing Your Mindset

Your body is a natural wealth of information, so we're going to play with both tuning and tapping into that innate intelligence. I want you to notice how your body feels with each example and where you feel more or less energized.

Scenario

You work very hard at your job but have a difficult time getting raises or are passed over for promotions.

What do you tell yourself?

A. It's not fair. I'm not seen as the leader I know I am. I can't stand the way this office works! My CEO, Jennifer, definitely likes my colleagues better. I'm going to start my job search since I'm not good enough for her.

B. I'm upset that I've not been asked to take on more exciting projects. I wonder if there's something I've been doing or not doing to cause my manager not to see my value? I know she wants the best for our firm, and I want to make a difference and contribute. I am going to see if I can chat with her to inquire how I can improve.

Awareness of one's true abilities and reflection on possible steps produces a more positive outlook. You can practice holding a positive outlook by reframing situations so that you are back in charge of your next actions and steps. Yes, life really works this way. We go through each situation constantly making meaning of all that's happening around us.

Remember this **STAR** equation: S + T + A = R. The Situation + your Thoughts and feelings + your Actions = your Results. In other words, we interpret a situation and come up with thoughts about it (often judging it in some way versus seeing it as neutral), which provokes feelings that then contribute to our actions. Those actions produce your results. Whether you've been told by your peers that you are too talkative or need to have more empathy, the words you use to interpret the situation will ultimately affect your results and success.

As you practice using new words, I'd strongly encourage you to practice listening to the words you say to yourself and to others. The clues are all there. The more you get in tune with your body and how you perceive your life situations, the more you'll be able to feel how certain words support affirmative steps and outcomes. Learning to tune into your body is a powerful and free tool that is always available to you.

Let's put this in real time with your everyday job.

Write down an area where you feel stuck or frustrated.

_____

_____

_____

_____

What did or do you tell yourself about this situation?

_____

_____

_____

_____

Now list new ways to view this same situation. Try to create at least two positive points of view.

- One new way to view this situation is:

_____

_____

_____

- A second perspective on this situation is:

_____

_____

_____

- A third perspective on this situation is:

_____

_____

_____

- A fourth perspective on this situation is:

_____

_____

_____

_____

- The brand-new view I am open and eager to try is:

_____

_____

_____

_____

Look at your first response and check in to see how that made you feel.

- Are you more or less energized?

- Are you inspired to take action?

- Do you want to crawl into a fetal position?

Now, check your responses for the next four outlooks. Can you see a correlation between the words you use and the way you interpreted the situation?

We often have to create new ways to look for a new perspective. Consider that the words we use are one of the key things that keep us stuck or, conversely, helps us to feel courageous, empowered, and willing to change.

You, too, can welcome growth and learning opportunities that help you to develop more endurance, resilience, strength, and grit.

"When you change the way you look at things,
the things you look at change."

~ESTHER HICKS,

Ask and It Is Given: Learning to Manifest Your Desires

Practice in the Present

A few years ago, I was stuck on the road during an extensive and pretty frightening snowstorm with about 2 percent visibility. I was anxious, annoyed, and scared to drive, to the point where I almost pulled over. After taking a few deep breaths, saying a few prayers, and calling my husband to vent, I reminded myself that this was an awesome opportunity to both appreciate the abundance of snow and learn how to drive successfully in any terrain and weather. I felt my body relax and let go. I put on some meditative music and drove about three miles per hour with the belief that I was gaining a new skill. Granted, it took me two hours to travel five miles, but I came away feeling lit up and grateful to be alive.

A Seven-Day Word Exercise

To help get yourself in the habit of practicing positive words, jot down or record the unhelpful/non-supportive words you use with others as well as what you tell yourself. I'd recommend getting a small journal or finding a good recording app so you don't forget if you don't have this book handy when it happens.

For example, write down when you say something about yourself, like, "I'm an idiot for forgetting my keys."

Next, write down how that made you feel, such as annoyed, jealous, less-than, excited, motivated, eager.

Lastly, write down a new positive way to talk to yourself. Try it out now.

Write something negative you said to yourself recently:

_____

_____

_____

_____

How does that make you feel?

_____

_____

_____

_____

What is a positive phrase you could say instead?

_____

_____

_____

_____

How does that make you feel?

_____

_____

Keep at it. My hunch is that you will start to notice a pattern in your speech. The intention is to increase your awareness of what you are actually saying to yourself and to others about yourself. Interrupting negative self-talk helps you take charge of how you feel about yourself and what you are capable of.

Don't forget that our bodies are *always listening*. I'll never forget the moment I learned that our gut has more sensory neurons than our brain. The gut is often referred to as the second brain. I would invite you to consider that our bodies and minds are way more intertwined than we can fathom. Just knowing scientifically that our gut is linked to our brain hopefully gives some possibility to see this connection. I mention this to drive home the point again about watching our words. As the author and motivational speaker Mike Dooley says, "Thoughts become things."

The World of AND

I'm now going to introduce you to one of my favorite words of all time. It's a simple, three-letter word that changed my life. That word is simply: *and*. I learned from practice that swapping the word *but* with *and* could change my world. It's astounding, and it's been a game changer for me. Listen to yourself and become the "But Special Ops Force." When you use the word *but*, you're inherently saying that there's only room for one way to do something. It squashes out any possibility.

For example, "I want to take a break today during work to meditate and de-stress, *but* my day is too jam-packed with urgent and important work to do." In that statement, you've already decided there's no room to pause, breathe and get still. Using the word *but* gives you an out. But try this (pun intended) instead: "I have a jam-packed day with lots to accomplish, *and* I will find a way to incorporate a short meditation so I can stay calm and grounded." You still might choose not to meditate; however, by using *and*, you are creating a possibility to get your butt on a chair, mat or floor to meditate.

Let's try another real-life example that comes up for me all the time: "I need more sleep, *but* there's a lot to do at night after the kids go to sleep," can become "I need a lot more sleep, *and* there's a lot to do at night after the kids go to bed." See the difference? In the first example, it seems impossible to get more sleep. The door is closed, it's not happening, there is too much to do. You just wrote off any chance of seeing where you can tweak your schedule. In the second sentence, the word "and" allows for the potential to get more sleep *and* do chores after the kids go to sleep. Using the word "and" creates potentiality and possibility. It might seem like a small thing, but I can assure you that this three-letter word is a game changer.

Can you imagine how often we limit ourselves with our words? Start taking note of when you say "but" and replace it with "and" to see how you feel afterward. You're also going to start noticing where and when others use the same limiting language. You will notice yourself taking empowering new actions and becoming more of the person you want to be.

Want to crush it in work and in life? Use the word *and* as often as possible.

Following is a fun list of words and phrases to use in the place of ones that don't serve your highest potential. I challenge you to become your own word investigator. When these less-than-kind words pop up, know you're headed to the limited-thinking zone. The quickest way to adjust your course is to change your words and, as a result, redirect your thoughts. Don't forget the **STAR** equation: Situation + Thoughts and feelings + Actions = Results.

Here are some new affirming words and phrases to try on:

Instead of:	Say this:
Failure	Learning opportunity
But	And

Crisis	Growth opportunity
Perfection	Focused to do my best
I'm unable	I don't know how yet
I'm trapped	Another way has yet to be disclosed
I never have	I have yet to do this
I never will	All is possible
I can't picture it	I'm open and willing to picture it
I am always the one who	I'm willing to let go of thoughts of being the victim that don't help me or others
I'm an idiot	I am constantly learning from all situations
Can't	Not yet
Won't	Perhaps someday
I'm too busy	My life is full
Why me?	What can I learn here?
This happened to me again	What do I need to change to alter this outcome?
I have to	I get to

Keep the list going. What other words can you add here?

Your turn.

Download these affirming words and phrases to keep them top of mind at **juliereisler.com/masteryourself.**

Instead of:	Say this:

Getting Out of the Victim Zone

Did you notice during this activity that new awareness surfaces from a hard experience? In the past, you might have allowed that uncomfortable or upsetting situation to keep you in a victim mentality. But now, you can see that something in that experience allowed you to open your mind to a new perspective. Being open, even to a small degree, to greater understanding allows you to perceive the situation differently. Train yourself to ask, "How can I learn from this experience?" This will always lead to new awareness, learning, and growth. This kind of openness creates a much different experience than complaining, "Why does this always happen to me?" or "When will I find the right person?" In other words, you're learning to sift for the teachable moment and change your mindset.

Now let's pull back the curtain and put this into practice with a mindset shift activity.

> When something happens that you do not like, or if you feel like you failed, ask yourself: "Where can I take responsibility? How might I see this differently? What's a new awareness with this experience?"

_____

_____

_____

_____

Other great awareness-provoking questions include the following:

How can I learn from this situation?

_____

_____

_____

_____

What do I need to see that will help me shift my perspective?

_____

_____

_____

What is it that I need to focus on or do right now?

What might be the gift here?

Check in with yourself here. What did you learn from this activity? What shift happened mentally, emotionally or with your energy level? Use this as data to track internal changes and growth.

 "All of our words evoke, develop, and bring forth our reality. We always have the power to choose our words and thus our reality."

~JULIE REISLER

Homework: Chapter 5

Accountability & Team Check-in Reminder

Daily Review:

1. Light-bulb moments or new awareness

2. An action you committed to taking that day correlating to a new habit you are forming

3. Three things you're grateful for

Self-Reflection Journal Space

Write about the negative things you say aloud or tell yourself silently. For example, write down when you say something like, "I'm an idiot for forgetting my keys." Next, write down how that made you feel, such as being annoyed, frustrated, or less-than. The intention is to increase your awareness of what you are actually saying to yourself, as well as to others about yourself, and think about how those words make you feel. Then replace those words and statements with positive alternatives.

Writing prompt: If you want some help focusing on what you learned in this chapter, you can use these writing prompts to begin.

- When I look at the tough situations in my life, I realize that...

- I can see the growth opportunity in this situation...

MODULE THREE:

DIRECTION

Chapter Six

BE THE CEO OF YOUR CAREER

"The best way to predict the future is to create it."

~PETER DRUCKER

What does it mean to be the CEO of your career? Is this something you strive for? Whether or not you ever desire to be a Chief Executive Officer at work, the concept focuses on the fact that you are always in the driver's seat of your career—and your life—regardless if you like it. In fact, whether you are consciously choosing the direction you want to head in or you are going along with the current, you are still going somewhere. This chapter is about examining where you are headed, identifying stories that might get in the way and those that empower you, and determining what will aid you as you create a career and life in the direction of your greater vision.

Even though this section is focused on the future, it's crucial to understand that most of us are creating our future based on past stories and beliefs.

"Within our dreams and aspirations, we find our opportunities."
~SUE ATCHLEY EBAUGH

Choose Your Story

As human beings, we are constantly trying to find meaning by making up stories about the world around us. Throw in the propensity for the human brain to focus on negatively slanted stories, known as the *negative bias*, and we're left with a whole slew of stories that often don't help us live out our potential. Here's the other interesting thing to understand: your past life events are concrete, but how you interpret those events are not. Would you like some help with this? If so, go here: juliereisler.com/you-me

Given that there are infinite ways to make meaning of our life occurrences, every person will have a different interpretation of the same events. You're probably used to seeing your version of your story as the truth. Here's the rub—phenomena (observable events like who, what, when, how, and where) and the story (the meaning you assign to the experience) are not the same and have infinite interpretations. This is good news, actually. If you're willing and open-minded, there are always new ways to view an experience.

For example, my client Cara failed her real estate exam. The phenomena are that she studied for, took, and failed the exam. Cara's story around those events is that *she is a failure and will never be able to help clients buy their dream home*. It's easy to see how we can get very stuck in our particular stories and limit our ability for infinite possibilities.

Here's another example of perspective. Let's say I'm looking to change jobs or get back into the career force. I'm on a mission to interview with my top three companies. I wake up early, meditate, eat a good breakfast, get dressed for my interview, get in the car and realize I forgot my resumé. I am in the car realizing I didn't bring my resumé or any ID, and then I get lost on the way to the interview. I finally find the correct turn and have trouble finding parking. I'm starting to feel that this interview is not going to work out well (story one). In fact, I'm now pretty sure that my chances of getting this job are slim to none (more dramatic story). The cards feel stacked against me (more of the same old negative story).

I'm going to pause here to consider two possible outcomes. If I continue running with my storyline of "everything is going wrong and I'm doomed," guess what my interview experience will be? We know that our beliefs and internal state are contagious. It's guaranteed that when I go in with the belief that I'm not good enough, I'll be frustrated, negative, and certainly convince my potential new employers that I shouldn't land the job. However, if I can see that I'm starting to weave a pretty compelling "woe is me" story, I can stop in my tracks, affirm that I can be creative about forgetting my resumé, perhaps by figuring out a way to pull it up online and assuming that they are going to see how passionate I am about their company.

Another thing that can shift you into a positive state is using your breath and movement. Changing your condition—be it getting up and jumping a few times, taking a quick walk or getting into a victory pose with your arms held high—can alter your energy and emotional states. We will address this in detail in Chapter Seven.

I know from personal experience that what I tell myself and how I assess a situation (positive vs. negative) *will* determine how my message is delivered, how I'm interacting with others, how my impact is received and how my career unfolds. If you want to see what thoughts and stories you're telling yourself, look at what's happening right now in your career. Do you feel like you are getting new and fascinating projects? Do you feel overlooked? Are you stagnant and frustrated? Are you feeling challenged and pushed to expand?

A lot of feeling frustrated, stuck, trapped, insecure, resentful, and stressed is based on how we interpret past events. Once you realize you have total control over how to interpret your work and life situations, it's just a matter of time before you will start to act like the CEO of your career.

As the CEO of YOU, you can always choose new perspectives and stories that will leave you feeling empowered, uplifted and inspired. In this chapter, you'll learn how to tap into your internal navigation system that can help you to drive in the direction of where you want to go.

Connecting the DOTS

Consider that we all have a **Default Operating and Tracking System**, or **DOTS** for short. Our DOTS represent our modus operandi: how we function, track, and make meaning of past events, interpret the future, and metaphorically connect these dots.

In order to connect these dots, we have to first understand that our current beliefs and stories—especially if not checked out, reviewed, reappraised, and consciously questioned—are based on our environment, culture, and often our upbringing. Whether they come from our former boss, past workplace, parents, friends, peers, societal programming, education system, first breakup, religion, first love, or any of the varied experiences encountered over one's life events, the good news is that you can change your DOTS at any time.

Another way to look at your DOTS is to examine your typical mindset. Do you tend to be in a fixed or growth mindset? Carol Dweck explains the difference powerfully in her book, *Mindset*. In essence, a growth mindset is where you are open to change, comfortable with making mistakes and see failure as an opportunity to learn and grow. A fixed mindset is one in which perfectionism prevails and failure should be avoided at all costs. Guess which one leads to satisfaction, innovation, and success in the workplace? While the answer is obvious, changing from a fixed to a growth mindset is not always obvious.

Your biggest challenge can become your greatest strength if you choose to look at it through that lens.

It's now time for you to connect *your* DOTS.

Dismantling and rewriting your stories allows the restorative power of awareness and understanding to work on releasing limiting thoughts. This process allows you to be CEO—in this case, Chief Empowerment Officer—of your career.

Thank you for being bold enough to look at yourself and to see where you can make a change.

We bring limiting beliefs into the light by choosing to take a look at what's hiding in the dark corners of our unconscious minds. You can do this on your own, through a book like this or along with accountability partners to share the process with you.

We have all acquired and made up stories that don't serve our true greatness. Know that looking at your stories head-on can feel uncomfortable at first. It's not uncommon to experience pain, disappointment, and frustration when you let go of old beliefs in order to rewire your brain for new thought patterns and stories. Breaks in patterns and breakdowns lead to breakthroughs.

"Connect the dots between individual roles and the goals of the organization. When people see that connection, they get a lot of energy out of work. They feel the importance, dignity, and meaning in their job."

~KEN BLANCHARD

DOTS Assessment

In order to get a sense of some of your DOTS, let's look at how you view these specific areas of your career and life.

Following are some questions to ask yourself.

What is my core belief about my career? (Such as: "It all works out in the end," "Work is a crazy ride and I'm not the driver," "If I work hard enough, everything is possible," "The world is an impersonal place," or "I'm not destined to be promoted.")

_____

_____

_____

_____

How did this core belief develop? (Did I adopt it from my family, education, past work experience, community, or financial history?)

_____

_____

_____

_____

Do I have any explicit memories around these five areas that could have shaped my perspective? When did they happen, who was involved, and what idea or belief emerged from the experience?

1. Family (Example: *My mom didn't get her dream job until she was forty years old. She taught me that when you believe in yourself and are persistent, with a passion to keep learning, anything is possible.*)

_____

_____

2. Career (Example: *I've never been able to hold down a job, so I'm worried I'll always hop from job to job with no stability.*)

3. Spirituality (Example: *My spirituality leads me to believe that wanting "too much" money or success in my career is greedy and selfish.*)

4. Health and well-being (Example: *Working too hard in the past left me stressed and burnt out, to the point of developing an ulcer.*)

5. Relationships (Example: *My dad constantly jumped from job to job, always starting a new business, with very little financial security and stability. It affected his relationship with my mom and us kids, as we barely saw him. I learned that being an entrepreneur could be risky. I had to really address this story before becoming an entrepreneur myself.*)

Trying on a New View

It's okay to have something come up that you realize doesn't truly represent how you want to think or how you want to be in the world. This is actually a great place to be. We can't change without awareness, so we need to see what's going on before we can make a shift.

This showed up for me around spreadsheets and creating systems, as I was not particularly strong at detailed tracking systems or mastering numbers. In my former 9-5 day job, I was the director of recruiting for a successful Fortune 500 restaurant chain. Part of my job was to track all of the candidates, the recruiters we worked with, the recruiting costs and other details necessary to maintain a robust new-hire database. I had made many mistakes in Excel and thought I had exhausted the accounting team, who tirelessly showed me how to create tracking systems that would make the process easier. I found it frustrating and not an area I wanted to focus on. While tracking data and numbers is not my favorite task, I learned from this experience that I could become proficient at anything I focused on. I changed the story about myself and realized that I could focus on projects that required me to do tracking and accounting. This allowed me to create an opportunity to learn something new and expand my toolbox. This example might sound minor, but I can assure you that the amount of energy I wasted on avoidance and being annoyed was not worth it. Changing my perspective freed my energy and time and also helped me to learn a new skill set.

This is just one small example of what happens when you start seeing how your stories about who you are can clearly affect your work, your ability to climb the ladder in your career, your relationships, your vision for yourself, and your life as a whole.

"All dreams come true if we have the courage to pursue them."
~WALT DISNEY

Stories to Help You Crush It

OK, enough examples. It's time to rewrite your story. Yup, you are going to craft the story you would like to live out in your career. This is an opportunity to dream, envision and write out your goals, think expansively, and map out what your work life will look like one, three, five, ten, and fifteen years from now.

Ready to give it a go? Since you now know we are all creating stories, I want you to think about what you'd like your new story to look like. Take time and space here to write it out. What's the best from your past that you want to bring forward in your future? What are the values, characteristics, traits or ideals that are non-negotiable for your future story?

Remember, this is your career, your next chapter, and your story that you get to create.

"The future belongs to those who believe
in the beauty of their dreams."

~ELEANOR ROOSEVELT

What's the best from your past you want to bring forward in your future?

_____

_____

_____

_____

What are the values, characteristics, traits or ideals that are non-negotiable for your future story?

_____

_____

_____

_____

The next step would be to create a shared imagined future and collective story to level up the inner workings within your organization. See the bonus chapter for more information on how to do this.

"When we choose to shift our thoughts, beliefs,
and habits, the world seems to positively shift around us."

~JULIE REISLER

Homework: Chapter 6

Accountability & Team Check-in Reminder

Daily Review:

1. Light-bulb moments or new awareness

2. An action you committed to taking that day, correlating to a new habit you are forming

3. Three things you're grateful for

Self-Reflection Journal Space

Use your journal space to affirm what you are realizing and learning about yourself. Note what you have learned about your current DOTS (Default Operating and Tracking System) and how you would like to change this mental system so you are more conscious.

Writing prompt: If you want some help focusing on what you learned in this chapter, you can use these writing prompts to begin.

• A new story I'm eager to write about my career is...

• What I learned about my DOTS is...

_____

_____

_____

_____

Chapter Seven

HARNESSING YOUR ENERGY 101

"Energy and persistence conquer all things."
~BENJAMIN FRANKLIN

I 'd argue that we as individuals, and thus as a collective, are in a serious energy emergency, and in this chapter, I'm not talking about energy derived from oil, solar power or electric energy. I'm referring to our own internal energy system.

You don't have to read stats or dig through data to know this. Look at yourself and your peers. Unless you are actively managing your energy (kudos if you are), many of us are energy depleted, be it from stress, lack of proper nutrition or exercise, not enough sleep, improper handling of emotions like fear, overwhelm, and doubt or living on autopilot. I was influenced by and greatly affected after reading about the findings from the *Harvard Business*

Review article, "Manage Your Energy Not Your Time," by Tony Schwartz and Catherine McCarthy in the October 2017 issue. You can read more evidence about the human energy crisis in this article.

*"Energy, not time,
is the fundamental currency of high performance."*
~TONY SCHWARTZ

Spoiler alert: you can change and manage your energy to heal from or hopefully avoid a full-out energy emergency. Change is possible. Read on to better understand how energy affects all aspects of our career and our life.

Let's look at how science defines energy. In physics, energy is expressed as the capacity to work. It can be expressed in thermal, solar, electrical, chemical, potential, and nuclear forms. Both force and acceleration affect the amount of energy needed and used.

Within the human system, energy can be connected to and found within your body, mind, emotions, and purpose. While we have a fixed amount of energy in each of these areas, there are natural and intrinsic ways to renew, expand, and restore energy. The goal is to tap into your biological energy sources and change energy-depleting habits to raise your energy and get positive results in your career and your life. It's tough to truly work at capacity if you are lacking energy. The aim here is to go from energetic surviving to energetic thriving.

To create more energy and reenergize yourself, you must look at both energy-giving and energy-depleting behaviors that can affect your well-being, attention, focus, productivity, stress level and satisfaction.

I invite you to look at energy from the perspective of nourishment, particularly how we nourish these four areas: **physical, mindset, emotional state and deeper connection.**

"To be fully engaged, we must be physically energized, emotionally connected, mentally focused, and spiritually aligned with a purpose beyond our immediate self-interest."

-JIM LOEHR

Physical Energy

Human stress levels seem to be at an all-time high, with many of us tethered to our email 24/7 and working longer hours than ever before. We know that excess stress leads to overproduction of the hormones adrenaline and cortisol, which are important if you are in a "fight or flight" situation since they give us that extra energy and the jolt we need to run, flee, or handle an emergency situation. However, repeatedly flooding our internal nervous and endocrine systems with these hormones when there is not a real physical threat can lead to major depletion in our energy. This depletion often translates into dis-ease within the body, causing many of the ailments known to be linked directly to stress, like high blood pressure, compromised immune system, anxiety, and lack of sleep. It can eventually lead to major illnesses like heart disease, stroke, and autoimmune conditions such as diabetes, underactive and overactive thyroid, irritable bowel syndrome (IBS) and Crohn's disease, just to name a few.

Stress also is a major cause for the high obesity rate in America, and there is significant evidence that while under continued perceived stress, our bodies produce extra leptin, which is a hormone made by the adipose (fat) cells that cause the body to regulate fat production. Unfortunately, one of the easiest and most accessible ways to handle stress is to overeat, especially the foods that give you a rush of dopamine (the "good feeling" hormone). As you might be aware, the obesity rates are at an all-time high, with 35 percent of the U.S. population being obese.

Sadly, most of the foods we're eating are lacking in any real nutrients, especially in most readily accessible food products. Much of our food sources are stripped of nourishing minerals, vitamins, and other healing properties. And then there's the overuse of sugar, known to cause inflammation, trigger an addictive response, and negatively affect gut health.

I'd say that our physical nourishment is in a crisis. You can thank your brain in part for this relationship to food.

I've seen this detriment in my own life as someone who has struggled with food and sugar addiction. Even if you are not addicted, per se, to sugar, there's a reason you might grab the candy from your colleague's candy dish over and over again after promising yourself not to. Sugar in particular triggers the same reward center part of our brain as opioids, alcohol, and sex. This is the "feel good" part of the brain that responds immediately to these "drugs" by giving you a hit, or a rush of relaxation and happy feeling. A way to curb this habit, especially in the workplace, is to learn the power of the 'Mind Pause'. We'll dive into that shortly.

But first, let's talk about how you are fueling your body. What if you thought of fueling your body like filling a gas tank? Ideally, you wouldn't repeatedly drive until your tank was so empty your car dies because, after so many instances, your car will likely break down. The same thing happens to our body.

How about physical movement? How, if at all, are you moving your body? Did you used to play high school or college sports only to find yourself now sitting at your desk for more than eight hours a day with little movement other than to type an email, swipe your phone, or reach for a snack? Movement is crucial to restoring energy, and most of us miss golden opportunities to add movement to our workday. As you know, exercise has loads of benefits for your brain, lungs, heart, and muscle tissue. Regular movement will also improve your posture, along with your ability to focus, lose weight, and sleep better.

If you are committed to feeling better and being more productive, focused, and thriving at work, I'd recommend looking at creatively adding movement.

This can mean taking the stairs instead of the elevator; dedicating five minutes each morning and afternoon to do a few planks, squats and stretches; or doing a walking meeting with your colleague. If you are working for a company, they might have free or discounted memberships at a local gym. Find out about your corporate wellness plan to see what you can leverage and take advantage of. Get into the habit of asking yourself: "What does my body need? Do I need more sleep? What foods would give me more energy? What kind of movement would be best for my body?"

Adding movement will pay dividends in your energy bank. Any kind of movement will help keep you feeling more uplifted and nourished inside and out.

<u>Renewed Energy Action</u>: Commit to and choose at least one thing below you will incorporate into your working schedule to enhance your physical energy:

- Find twenty minutes per day for movement at work (walking meeting, stretches, mini workouts, taking the stairs)

- Get in 10,000 steps at work using a fitness tracking device

- Drink three liters of water each day

- Get at least seven to eight hours of sleep every night

- Eat five to eight servings of vegetables each day

- Cut out all processed food for one week and note how you feel

- Keep sugar to a minimum, no more than five grams per serving or at a given meal, and keep track of how you feel

- Pause for five minutes before eating seconds of anything

Mindset Strategies

How you care for and tend to your mind is crucial. You must mind your mind.

In Hal Elrod's book, *The Miracle Morning*, he notes that whether we realize it or not, we design our lives in each moment by the thoughts and actions we choose. After gathering data from the most successful leaders, performers, and entrepreneurs, Hal found the six common practices that lead to success and restored energy. He recommends devoting an hour every morning to these six practices called the S.A.V.E.R.S., which stands for Silence (meditation or prayer), Affirmations, Visualization, Exercise, Reading (something inspirational) and Scribing (journaling). Each habit alone can change your mental state enough to affect your thoughts, which then create your feelings, actions, and results.

To home in on the importance of adding silence or meditation, studies show that we can alter our ability to pause, make better choices at the moment, and handle stress through mindfulness and taking breaks.

The Power of the Mind Pause

Adding a "pause" button in my life has been a game-changer.

We are all born with the capacity to know what we innately need. Somehow we lose touch with this, and we take on bad habits that aren't truly nourishing. Learn to be more mindful and take mind pauses. Set aside pauses throughout your day for 'Power Minutes'. It might mean sitting at your desk, closing your eyes and focusing on your breathing for one minute. Set a timer for different times throughout the day to close your eyes, focus on your breathing, practice gratitude, do affirmations and recommit to your goals. Studies show that when we sit still and breathe, we retrain our brain to increase our ability to react with intention. Maybe you just received an assignment that you know is going to take a lot of time and focus, and which might not be one of your favorite assignments. Before diving in—and allowing overwhelming and stressful thoughts to take over—it is helpful to pause and take a few deep breaths to allow for more oxygen in your lungs and the space to get perspective. Training yourself to take a quick *mind pause* and do your 'Power Minutes' retrains your brain to handle stressful situations with the practice of stopping to breathe deeply and reframe. And, note to all: it costs you or your company nothing to pause and breathe.

Meditation and mindfulness practices also help you to be more compassionate to yourself and empathetic to others. Empathy is one of the key success components identified as necessary for being a strong leader.

"When you show deep empathy toward others,
their defensive energy goes down, and positive energy
replaces it. That's when you can get more creative in solving problems."
~STEPHEN COVEY

For those who are still on the fence or unsure about meditation or mindfulness, it is simply being still, breathing, and focusing your attention on the present moment. As thoughts come and go, just gently detach and go back to your breath. You should expect your mind to wander, to have ongoing and random thoughts. That will not change since as human beings our brain is designed to think (approximately 70,000 thoughts per day). The real effects show up and are recognized when you are not in meditation. When I meditate regularly, I can feel a huge change in my stress response, and a big bonus is my ability to handle challenging and stressful work situations with ease.

"Between stimulus and response, there is a space.
In that space is our power to choose our response.
In our response lies our growth and our freedom."
~VIKTOR FRANKL, Holocaust Survivor

<u>Renewed Energy Action</u>: Commit to and choose at least one thing below you will incorporate into your working schedule to enhance your mind energy:

- Start with a five-minute meditation before your workday begins (there are many ways to do this, none being right or wrong; a great app to find any meditation you can imagine is Insight Timer, and it's free).

- Create powerful affirmative phrases that inspire and motivate you. Read these every morning and before you go to bed.

- Set your alarm to take one-minute *mind pauses* every hour.

- Take a quick walk outside to change your scenery, get fresh air and gain a new perspective.

Emotional State

In addition to nourishing your physical body and mindset, you must also create space to handle and express your emotions in a healthy manner; otherwise, your issues could end up in your (bodily) tissues.

 "In times of great stress or adversity, it's always best to keep busy, to plow your anger and your energy into something positive."

—LEE IACOCCA

We know scientifically that our mind and body are connected. Unresolved feelings like deep sadness, shame or anger can lead to a lack of well-being. How we express and handle our emotions is directly related to how we interact with our colleagues. The study of Emotional Intelligence (EQ) by Daniel Goleman shows that well-being and managing of one's feelings is connected to success in the workplace. It makes sense if you think about it; I can't imagine you'd want to work with someone who is passive aggressive, negative, or blaming everyone else. If you are feeling stuck with certain emotions that don't feel productive or good to you, it's probably an indication that your emotional energy system is clogged. A way to shift this and add restoration is to find a way to safely and effectively feel and release these feelings. That could mean working with a mentor, coach, counselor, or trusted friend.

Remember, you bring your whole self to work. If there is an area of your life that is not working the way you want it to, it's prudent to take a closer look to see how you can address and work through your situation. A phrase I like to use is that you've got to "feel to heal." I think many of us try not to experience feelings that don't feel good, or we're conditioned by our family or society to avoid expressing "negative" feelings. Often, these emotions are trying to send you a message, like an emotional text message aiming to grab your attention. Listen in and give your feelings the respect they deserve. If they feel like too much to handle, that could be a good time to see a professional therapist or psychiatrist.

Another aspect of cultivating positive emotional energy and well-being is in regard to living your purpose. When I think of purpose, I think about the intersection between your innate strengths and skills with what gives you a feeling of being of service and making an impact and significant difference.

What do you feel naturally skilled at? What do you enjoy doing, so much that you would perhaps do it for free? Where do you feel most connected to your authentic purpose? What are you most passionate about?

"Passion is energy. Feel the power that comes from focusing on what excites you."
~OPRAH WINFREY

<u>Renewed Energy Action</u>: Commit to and choose at least one thing below you will incorporate into your working schedule to enhance your emotional energy:

- Give yourself space to feel your emotions. A great way to do this is through journaling.

- Hire a coach or counselor to work with you through an emotional landmine.

- Ask someone you admire at or outside of work to be your mentor.

- What is your career "why?" Write it out and look at it every day.

- Make sure to incorporate at least one top strength each day at work and home.

Making Deeper Connections

A clue to uncover your purpose or deeper connection is to inquire about what aspects of your work give you energy. Whatever gives you energy is your body's natural way of telling you to do more of that thing. Your purpose gets to the heart of your "why," because it is what makes you feel and come most alive. When you feel alive, you thrive.

Human connection is another area often put to the side in our fast-paced world. There's an abundance of research on the importance of human connection, social bonds, and being able to chart goals and discuss your purpose with a trusted mentor or coach. Nourishing your innate need for connection can be part of your path to fulfilling your purpose and increasing your emotional energy. Ask yourself, "What are the ways that I feel deeply connected both to myself, to others and to my career?" Perhaps deeper connection means attending a spiritual or religious service, walking in nature, having an in-depth conversation with a close friend or peer, being part of a community service project or finding ways to volunteer and give back. It's worth the time investigating what gives you a feeling of deeper meaning, both in and out of work. Use the suggestions below to see what would provide a deeper meaning for you.

"When people go to work,
they shouldn't have to leave their hearts at home."

~BETTY BENDER

<u>Renewed Energy Action</u>: Commit to and choose at least one thing below you will incorporate into your working schedule to enhance your deeper connection energy:

- Find ways to volunteer, give back, and make a difference.

- Attend a group or service that fits your spiritual, religious and/or connection needs.

- Start a PhD in YOU group with your peers. For more information on this, including a how-to-guide, go here: juliereisler.com/groupguide

- Look for ways to find and express deeper connection every day.

Re-energize Yourself Inquiry

Consider the following questions:

1. What new mind-body connection action items are you willing to try?

_____

_____

_____

2. Can you add three to five minutes of meditation on a daily basis? When? (This is a free, small adjustment that will be a game changer.)

_____

_____

_____

_____

3. What kinds of nourishing foods will you make sure to eat? What are healthy foods you already like?

_____

_____

_____

4. What new physical activity do you want to try this week? Walking? Weight training? Yoga? Swimming? Biking? Stretching? Pilates?

_____

_____

_____

5. What about your relationship to your calendar and time management? Are you feeling like time is slipping by and you aren't sure where it is going? Is there a way to schedule five minutes a day to stretch, walk, add some lime to your water, or write a thank you note?

_____

_____

6. Is there someone whom you'd like to be your mentor or coach? Who can you reach out to and connect with? Don't wait—life is in the now.

"When you feel alive, you thrive."
~JULIE REISLER

Energy Begets Energy

Now that you've learned techniques to re-energize yourself you'll want to give it back to your team. After all, energy begets energy, creating a positive loop to elevate and inspire others around you.

Leadership consultants, Zoe Galvez and Betsy Crouch of ImprovHQ, bring improvisational theatre to business to spark cultures with creative energy. The principles of improv help teams with exceptional collaboration and effective communication while creating the bonds that help us all thrive. Work and play don't have to be mutually exclusive. They provide a guided series of activities and conversations that bring out the best in individuals and organizations. I have seen them transform groups in front of my own eyes. They have used these techniques to ignite teamwork on a whole other level with Fortune 500 companies like Google, Starbucks, Twitter and LinkedIn.

Use their I.M.P.R.O.V. principles, from their upcoming book, The Unscripted Leader, to energize your group and create deeper connections.

- **I**ntentional Listening -- elongate the moment of curiosity before jumping in with your thoughts.

- **M**ake your Teammate the Hero -- find ways to inspire and support your colleagues; simple things count.

- **P**ower of Presence -- Show up! Be in the moment.

- **R**esilient Response -- Call upon the best of yourself in the face of challenge. Find compassion for yourself and others when things don't go as planned.

- **O**pen to Yes -- Use "yes and" as a guideline to open up conversations and possibilities.

- **V**oice your Ideas -- celebrate diverse perspectives -- be bold and make room for others to also lean in.

It's amazing what's possible when you add fun and play!

"When you thrive, you ignite others to come alive."

~JULIE REISLER

Homework: Chapter 7

Accountability & Team Check-in Reminder

Daily Review:

1. Light-bulb moments or new awareness

2. An action you committed to taking that day, correlating to a new habit you are forming

3. Three things you're grateful for

Self-Reflection Journal Space

This week use your journal space to assess your own personal energy systems and where you would like more energy.

Writing prompt: If you want some help focusing on what you learned in this chapter, you can use these writing prompts to begin.

- I would like to cultivate more energy in the following area(s)...

- Ways I can do this are....

Chapter Eight

YOU CRUSHED IT!

CREATE, CATAPULT & CELEBRATE

"We think it's important for employees to have fun…
it drives employee engagement."

~TONY HSIEH, CEO of Zappos

You've come so far on your journey and you are practically ready for your final exam. But first, we're going to cover the Three C's: Create, Catapult & Celebrate.

Create the future you are aiming for because you now know you are in the driver's seat to steer your career to what's next.

Catapult by minding your mind and holding your goals close, and making sure to powerfully watch your thoughts, beliefs, and actions.

Celebrate! Because what's the point of doing all of this work without a big ole party at the end?

Create

Mindset Phrases

Mindset phrases are a great way to overwrite the human tendencies to believe the negative things our minds tell us.

Using powerful affirmative statements helps to put your goals and aspirations into motion and eventually bring them to reality.

There have been numerous leadership and business books written on the power of creating a vision—a road map of sorts—followed by affirmative statements. If you doubt the validity of this, I encourage you to think of a time when you've been in a sporting game, competition, or race of any kind. I'd imagine at some point, you envisioned how you wanted the outcome to go and probably said affirmative statements to yourself. The truth is, you are saying things to yourself all the time. Remember, approximately 70,000 thoughts run through our minds each day. That's a quite a few thoughts.

Powerful affirmative statements have worked impressively well for me and for many of my clients. In order to design and create your ideal future self at work, you'll want to get clear on what statements will support these goals coming to fruition.

Below is a list of some of my favorite statements.

Powerful Affirming Statements

- I am committed to using my strengths in all areas of work and life.

- I agree to take full 100 percent responsibility for all my actions and the results.

- Integrity is non-negotiable. I will follow through on my word.

- I choose to cultivate a positive mindset no matter what my work situation is, through reading and listening to inspirational material and saying my words with intention.

- I choose to give my colleagues the benefit of the doubt and be empathetic to their situation.

- What I appreciate appreciates. I cultivate an attitude of gratitude in all aspects of my work.

- I am the author of my career and choose to write an empowering story.

- I choose to see everything today as a growth and learning opportunity.

These statements are a starting point for you. Write down the top five powerful affirmative statements that resonate most strongly with you, or write your own. Tweak and edit as you see fit.

Catapult

Ready to soar? You are the only one who can make a change for yourself. Whenever you catch yourself saying something negative, replace it with something positive. Start developing your new habit pattern around affirming what you *do* want, not what you *don't* want. You can train your brain at any time to think in new ways. Remember, our brain is malleable, so we are always able to change it in a positive direction. The key is that change starts with you. Keep your top three powerful affirming statements with you and review them daily, either as a daily calendar reminder, notes in your workspace, or even as your screen saver. Every morning, I write my affirmation on a 3x5 card and carry it around with me. I use neon colored 3x5 cards so they are easy to find and I read them out loud when I'm waiting for something or someone, and as often as it occurs to me to do so during the day.

Celebrate

Powerful Practice: Celebrate the Wins

Find a reason each and every day to celebrate any win. We are wired to appreciate feeling appreciated. Learn to give appreciation to yourself first. Start a practice of celebrating the micro-steps and macro-leaps.

Growth is to be celebrated and valued because any change in a healthy direction, no matter how small, is an excellent shift. Your thoughts, beliefs, and actions create who you are and who you are becoming.

Most of us overlook this important daily practice, which can cost us moments of satisfaction, empowerment, and joy. Sometimes we tend to downplay our accomplishments or devalue our effect and impact. As you start to find wins to acknowledge daily, you will recalibrate your celebration mentality. More wins will come your way to recognize, and you'll find more to celebrate.

Celebration can be quite simple. It could be doing something intentionally nice for yourself, like giving yourself an extra ten minutes to chat with a colleague, enjoy your favorite tea or take yourself to your favorite lunch spot. You could also schedule a personal celebration. We're all unique, so this needs to be individualized.

Let's engage in a quick celebration inquiry.

What constitutes a celebration to you? When will you do this?

_____

_____

_____

_____

You could also celebrate a colleague. Set the intention to do something kind for someone else each day or to recognize when you do something kind naturally.

Part of your crushing it at work—and beyond—is knowing how to stop, have a laugh and acknowledge your wins and those of the people you work with. Celebration is a key to success in mastering both yourself and your career.

"Success is about knowing how to enjoy, celebrate and grow from any win."

~JULIE REISLER

Homework: Chapter 8

Accountability & Team Check-in Reminder

Daily Review:

1. Light-bulb moments or new awareness

2. An action you committed to taking that day, correlating to a new habit you are forming

3. Three things you're grateful for

Self-Reflection Journal Space

Use your journal space to reflect on how you're crushing it at work, how you've grown since working through this book and how you will celebrate your ongoing wins.

Writing prompt: If you want some help focusing on what you learned in this chapter, you can use these writing prompts to begin.

- I'm most excited about these wins:

- Ways that I'm now crushing it at work include:

- Ways I can celebrate a colleague are:

_____

_____

_____

_____

Congratulations! While your journey has just begun, it's time to celebrate and acknowledge your completion of *Get a PhD in YOU: Business Edition*. You can print the certificate here or at **juliereisler.com/certificate.**

PhD in

YOU:

Business Edition

CONGRATULATIONS

—————————————————————
Your Name

*You have taken the time, energy, and steps
to master yourself and crush it at work and in life.
Here's to your continued journey of personal
growth and development, and to your success!*

With gratitude,

Julie Reisler

Chapter Nine

GETTING A PHD IN YOU

AT THE SCALE OF ALL

A Bonus Chapter by Jon Berghoff

Jon Berghoff is not only one of the more brilliant minds I've been privileged to learn from, but he is also a heart centered leader committed to creating a new world focusing on and leveraging our strengths. Under Jon's leadership, the Flourishing Leadership Institute team has designed and facilitated whole-system change efforts through large group collaborative summits and programs for organizations that include BMW, Facebook, U.S. Army and Navy, Vitamix Corporation, and TEDx. Jon is a visionary, trailblazer, powerful facilitator and friend. I am thrilled to have Jon's wisdom in my book and to share his insights with you.

Getting a PhD in YOU represents a compelling opportunity that many of us are pulled toward. An invitation for us to ask the question—How might I connect to a deeper sense of purpose, my highest strengths, my best self, and ultimately bring forward a new vision for my future?

If you resonated with the fantastic journey Julie has taken you on, that's a credit both to the book and to you. Now, if any part of you wants to elevate and amplify this work to new levels of impact, I'm here with an invitation to do exactly that.

The provocative aim of this chapter is to raise the entire PHD framework to a new octave - from the micro to the macro. Here is why I'm such a huge fan of Julie's work. Her questions, artfully crafted to enable powerful individual-level transformation, deeply align with the primary question we've been asking for many years at the Flourishing Leadership Institute (FLI), aimed at group level transformation: What causes any human system—a team, organization, community, etc.—to come alive, more naturally, effectively, and faster than ever before?

If you are ready to manage and lead in a whole new way, let's explore how to bring the simple yet powerful PHD framework to the scale of an entire team, organization, or community - to any human system of any size.

Today, we are seeing some of the most advanced organizations, management and leadership practices are already using this PHD framework that you are holding in your hands, with a few simple tweaks, to enable large-scale transformations.

Here's just a few of the complex, high stakes environments we've seen this approach at work:

- leading the U.S. Navy through a 260-person, whole system planning summit to drive efficiencies, resulting in over 30 pilot projects and millions in savings

- facilitating a future visioning dialog with 500 CEO's at the United Nations (UN) Global Summit, that, according to scholar John Ruggie from Harvard, led the UN Global Compact to become the world's largest and most widely embraced corporate citizenship initiative with 13,000 corporate participants

- partnering with TEDx Traverse City to re-imagine the TEDx experience in ways that deeply engage the audience

- helping the self-driving division of BMW unlock collective intelligence across brilliant teams of engineers

- facilitating large groups at Facebook through complex collaborations among scientists, engineers, and researchers from around the world

- leading in the design and facilitation of the 4th Global Forum for Business as An Agent of World Benefit, where 400 global leaders, researchers, NGOs, and students from over 35 countries came to Case Western Reserve University to celebrate, create, and accelerate innovations aimed at solving the 17 United Nations Sustainable Development Goals

There are three governing principles for bringing the PHD framework into a group. As an added BONUS, we give you a sample facilitation guide for bringing this work to a group.

1. Inquiry as Intervention

2. Life-Giving Conversations

3. Experience of Wholeness

Principle 1: Inquiry as Intervention

"In the twenty-first century, knowing all the answers won't distinguish someone's intelligence – rather, the ability to ask all the right questions will be the mark of true genius."

-DR. JOHN KELLY III, IBM

The Power of Openness to Other Perspectives

Peter Senge's pioneering research and work on learning organizations and the importance of systems thinking as a critical discipline, reveals that one of the five critical factors in becoming a learning organization—an organization that is ultimately prepared to continually shape its own future in the face of complexity, change, and uncertain challenges—is the ability for members to evolve their own mental models. What does this mean in practical terms? In Senge's words, it's the ability to tilt the balance in our thinking and our conversations away from rigidly holding our perspectives toward an openness to alternative perspectives. Or, more simply put, it is the ability to balance "inquiry & advocacy".

The groundbreaking research from Marcial Losada and Barbara Fredericton have also confirmed this, when studying teams that perform at various levels. A leading indicator of high performing teams is the measured balance between inquiry and advocacy. In other words, it's crucial to train ourselves to be as open to new perspectives as we are interested in convincing others of our firmly held beliefs and opinions.

Our work in the field has shown this to be true time and again. Organizations, teams, and groups who are authentically curious consistently perform at high functioning levels. Consider this question: Are you, and those you work with, willing to step into your next conversations with a willingness to be influenced, just as much as you are aiming to influence? If so, this happens with both inquiry and advocacy or is it really just inquiry which connects back to your first principle.

Today at FLI, we hold the Theory U model of evolutionary social change as a guiding compass for our work. The Theory U Model, created by Otto Scharmer, asks us to "imagine a leap from our current Self to our emerging future Self. We are facing that threshold, gap, chasm, or abyss on all levels of scale: as individuals, groups, organizations, and as a global community. The question is, how can we activate our deeper levels of humanity in order to bridge and cross that divide?"[1] Theory U invites us to discover that when we see the world through the eyes of others we eventually connect to the present moment so deeply that we can begin to connect to the future as it is seeking to emerge.

With all the mounting evidence, why does it still remain difficult, even abnormal, for leaders to invite openness, inquiry, and the space to pause and listen? Why is it that managers consistently struggle to bring back the childlike curiosity, wonder, and humility to see anew?

Simple. Our egos, and our training, are clinging to old definitions of management and leadership - that managers should know what to do, where to go. If we are willing to accept that a new model for leadership is seeking to be born, we must start here, and be willing to tilt the scale towards inquiry.

A Story of Exponential Systemic Impact

In 2004, Professors David Cooperrider and Ron Fry of the Weatherhead School of Management at Case Western Reserve University (CWRU) proposed a powerful question about business as a force for good in the world:

Where might we search for, uncover, and ultimately help spread stories of businesses who have aligned their purpose with the most pressing problems and opportunities for solutions for a flourishing future of economic, social and environmental thriving?

Little did they know that their first question would be so fateful, it would eventually lead to the launch of the Aim2Flourish (A2F) initiative in 2015, based in the Fowler Center for Business as An Agent of World Benefit at CWRU.

In partnership with the United Nations (UN), A2F became the world's first higher education curriculum aimed at lifting the global story of business

---

1   *The Essentials of Theory U: Core Principles and Applications*, March 2018, Otto Scharmer

from best in the world to best for the world. Using Appreciative Inquiry, students search for and interview leaders of businesses who have created innovations that are supporting any of the 17 Sustainable Development Goals.

Today, Aim2Flourish proudly serves 400+ professors around the world, 6,200+ community members, 60 countries in our global community, 2,100+ business schools reached through participating education networks, and over 1,250 published Global Goals innovation stories. The power in the very first question asked, along with the gravitational pull of such a transcendent purpose, have led to what most would consider to be an exponential growth of this initiative since the June 2015 launch.

What was it about the first question that David and Ron posed that made it so powerful? Why is it that, once again, sparking collective curiosity became a tipping point capability?

> The questions we ask are fateful. Questions work like a lens, immediately changing how we see the world, even before the answers arrive.

While we continue to learn s about the power of inquiry, maybe the most important discovery is this:

Inquiry, when appreciative in nature, is the most potent source of intervention, in any human system—team, organization, or community.

Consider this discovery, that the questions we ask are fateful. Questions work like a lens, immediately changing how we see the world, even before the answers arrive. In this light, we see an emerging capability that leaders are being called to develop—the ability to ask the questions that bring out the best in an organization.

Principle 2: Life-Giving Conversations

"Look deep into nature, and then you will understand everything better."

~ALBERT EINSTEIN

A Lesson From Mother Earth

What if it's true, as organizational "future hacker" Bix Bickson suggests, that the DNA of any organizational culture lies inside of the conversations we have with each other? Creator of the SOAR framework (a positive approach to inquiry into strengths, opportunities, aspirations, and results for strategic conversations and planning), and FLI Senior Appreciative Inquiry Strategist Dr. Jacqueline Stavros, has inspired hundreds of organizational transformations over the last 20 years through strategic conversations that are appreciative, inquiry-based, and life-giving (www.soar-strategy.com).

As Jackie reveals in her most recent bestselling book, *Conversations Worth Having: Using Appreciative Inquiry to Fuel Productive and Meaningful Engagement*, the primary points of leverage for creating change are the conversations we have. Conversations lie at the heart of how we interact and impact others. As David Cooperrider says in the book "our organizational lives and the lives of others flourish or flounder one conversations at a time" (p.3). And of course, the fastest way to shift our conversations is through the questions we ask, both individually and systemically. Knowing this, we owe it to each other to become precision engineers of questions that lead to "life-giving" conversations that impact an environment to work for all.

As champions of Appreciative Inquiry (refer back to page 18 for more info on A.I.) as an "operating system" around the globe, FLI has had a privileged vantage point within organizations and communities that are choosing a strengths-based approach to conversation design. In 2017, our facilitators led in the design and facilitation of over 125 large group collaborations, with a total of over 25,000 individual conversations toward positive transformations happening within and across these organizational and community efforts. The measurable trajectory of outcomes—including the rapid shaping or creating of shared values, co-created visions, strategic initiatives, or highly focused solution designs—has been an astonishing affirmation that human beings are yearning for conversations that give life to them as individuals, and to their teams and organizations.

> In nature, life grows toward the sun. This is known as the Heliotropic Effect. What we are witnessing in organizations every day is the parallel expression of this living system principle—people are magnetically attracted, instantly energized, and creatively unleashed, when the conversations are designed to be "life-giving."

Four Naturally Life Giving Types of Questions

As conversation designers, engineers, and architects, we are continuously asking ourselves which questions bring out our best, most naturally, effectively and rapidly. At FLI, the following list of 4 'question types' represent some of the most common questions that form the beginnings of our large group collaboration work.

- **Purpose Questions**—Questions that invite us to connect to a deeper meaning, purpose, or fulfillment in general, or in relation to the meeting, event or task at hand.

  Why is this important? To you? To us? To the world?

  Why are we here?

  Why does this (work/project/task/team) matter?

Purpose Question Design & Facilitation Tips:

1. We begin nearly every engagement with a purpose question. The power of connecting first with the individual and collective "why," often brings a sense of meaning, fulfillment, and higher ground to the rest of the work we do.

2. Consider how valuable it is, for the members of a team, organization, or community to be meaningfully connecting over a purpose question, vs. the alternative where a leader, manager, or key executive is trying to convince everybody "why this matters."

- **Moments of Excellence Questions**—Questions that invite us to explore moments when we were at our best, either in general or in relation to the meeting, event, or task at hand.

  When is a story, a real example, of a time where we thrived? What was happening? What did you, others, and/or the organization contribute to this moment?

  What is an example that embodies when we have been at our best?

  When was a time when we excelled, as it relates to _____?

Moments of Excellence Question Design & Facilitation Tips:

1. It is very common for change efforts with groups to give the impression that we are changing because what we have done in the past is of no value. Moments of Excellence stories help us to reframe that our past is instead a source of wisdom, inspiration, and rich in learnings for our future.

2. Moments of Excellence stories shift the systemic communication mode from what is often "diagnostic" and based in constant "negotiation" to "dialogic" and based in co-shaping a new "narrative." This honors the learnings from Tom White, former executive for

GTE, where pioneering large scale change efforts were led with Appreciative Inquiry. Tom describes organizational culture as "the stories we tell about ourselves and our organization and then forget they are stories."

3. A Moment of Excellence story can be framed around any task or topic. If an organization wants to improve sales process, we can inquire into moments when our sales process was thriving. If we want to improve _____, what happens if we inquire into when we've been exceptional at _____, or, where we've seen other organizations who are exceptional at _____.

- **Continuity Questions**—Questions that invite us to uncover and clarify the strengths, values, or qualities of a system that we value the most. These are a way of honoring the strengths that, no matter how we change or evolve, will be nurtured, protected, and built upon as we shape a new future.

  What are all the qualities of our organization/team/community, processes, systems, products, etc. or general ways of operating that have contributed to our success in the past?

  No matter how we change or evolve, what qualities do we want to honor, preserve or protect, no matter where we go in the future?

  When we reflect on our "moments of excellence," what qualities do we see that we consistently brought to these moments?

  Continuity Question Design & Facilitation Tips:

  1. Mapping out the "core strengths" can be one of the most exhilarating and life giving conversations for a group. Keep in mind that these strengths can be referred to as "values," "guiding principles," "guiding strengths," or any other label that best serves.

2. Notice in our third sample question above, that a continuity question can explicitly build upon "moment of excellence" stories. We can study the success factors of our moments when we are at our best, to identify those qualities that we want to continue into the future.

3. Be sure to give time, not only for responses to a continuity question, but for a group to search for themes/patterns /and the commonalities, so that the collective strengths can move from being implicit to clearly communicated and explicit.

- **Future Image Questions**—Questions that invite us to see or stand in the future we most desire.

   It is five years from today and we have just awoken from a long sleep. As you look around, you see the organization/community that you have always wished and dreamed for. What is happening? How is the group different? What have we accomplished that gives you the greatest sense of pride, meaning, and fulfillment?

   Imagine five years from today, our organization has won an award for _____. What is being said about us? What are our customers, key partners, employees, and others saying about us?

Future Image Question Design & Facilitation Tips:

1. Jim Ludema, an Appreciative Inquiry consultant of 20+ years, teaches that organizations have a "dominant storyline" that shapes their perceptions and determines their patterns of action. When we invite group storytelling about the future, we not only ignite the human spirit of curiosity and creativity, but more importantly, we engender wide spread support and care for the future of the

organization. As we've learned from Margaret Wheatley, people "support what they create."

2. Co-creating shared visions is not about "common ground," finding what ideas are in common, but rather "higher ground," the ideas and possibilities that excite, inspire and compel action. When we lead strategic planning summits, it is important to not only assess "market value" (what is the potential for financial gain?), but "affinity value" (why do you like this idea? Does it excite you and call you to action? Will it inspire pride in you, the organization and key stakeholders) of a proposed strategy. This ensures that strategic decisions reflect both the organizational potential and the motivation to move ideas forward.[2]

3. When inviting groups to co-create shared visions of the future, invite the most creative, expressive possibilities for how the future is presented. Future cover stories of leading publications, award ceremonies, future skits/enactments, multi-dimensional representations of customer or organizational experiences, just to name a few. From physicians to factory workers to German engineers, we've learned to stop being surprised at how universally people desire to creatively express their hopes for the future.

For the curious minded, the two other types of questions that we did not explore here are "Design Questions" where we take future images and prototype actionable initiatives, and "Action/Commitment Questions" where we invite individual and collective action, towards shared possibilities that emerge in prior conversations.

---

[2]   *The Appreciative Inquiry Summit: An Emerging Methodology for Whole System Positive Change*, Diana Whitney, Ph.D., David L. Cooperrider, Ph.D.

Principle 3: The Experience of Wholeness

*"If there is one thing I've learned in my years on this planet,
it's that the happiest and most fulfilled people I've known
are those who devoted themselves to something bigger
and more profound than merely
their own self-interest."*

~JOHN GLENN

A Story of Unlocking Collective Intelligence

On February 21st, 2016, Lyell Clarke, CEO of Clarke, kicked off a whole-system appreciative inquiry strategic planning summit. He stood on a stage in front of 300 stakeholders, including all Clarke employees, customers, suppliers, researchers, and even a local group of high school students to bring in the voices of future generations.

To be clear, Lyell wasn't delivering a traditional presentation, speech, or mandate for the future of the organization. Instead, he presented a provocative, powerful invitation, via one question: How might we in this room, together, co-create the possibility for a bigger, braver, and bolder future that brings the Heart of Clarke to the world?

If anybody had any doubt as to whether or not systemic approaches to transformation can work, they only need to look at what happened the last time Clarke chose to bring Appreciative Inquiry in at the level of the whole system. At their 2012 Summit, focused on Accelerating Sustainability, a number of visions for the future organically emerged and strengthened, including

1. 50% reduction in waste

2. 25% reduction in carbon footprint and most audaciously

3. a headquarters of the future designed to LEED standards.

What happened? As of today, waste has been reduced by 64%, with 80% of all waste reused or recycled. The 264 tons of waste previously going to landfills has been reduced to 4 tons. Carbon footprint goals were achieved, using lower impact and electric vehicles, saving over $750K in operating costs in the process. Last, the grand idea that many admitted they thought would never happen—a headquarters of the future—became a reality within two years. The new HQ boasts open spaces, natural light, generates an excess of power through solar panels, and regenerates the surrounding natural ecosystems.

Given the high impact shared visions that came of the 2012 Clarke Summit, it's not a surprise that the following three aspirations emerged during their 2016 Summit, focused on becoming "Bigger, Braver, Bolder" as an organization:

1. Share the Heart of Clarke with the World

2. Become the Voice of the Industry

3. Become an Agent of World Health Benefit

These emergent ideas led to rapid collective action. First, the company as a whole chose to donate 1% of revenues, not profits, from its next generation products and services to environmental organizations around the world. Next, within 6 months of the summit, Clarke was invited to testify before U.S. Congress on how to better control Zika Virus. Finally, also within 6 months, Clarke sent 45 two-person crews to Miami Dade, to help stop transmission of Zika. Clarke's efforts contributed to this becoming the first time in history that local transmission of Zika was eradicated.

Unlike the long-held images of leadership as a heroic figure, Lyell, along with the support of Julie Reiter, VP of HR and Sustainable Development at Clarke, have long been modeling the redefinition of leadership toward a collective capacity versus an individual capacity. This is a key trend that Nick

Petrie, Senior Faculty member with the Center for Creative Leadership outlined in his 2014 report on Future Trends in Leadership:

If leadership is thought of as a shared process, rather than an individual skill set, senior executives must consider the best way to help leadership flourish in their organizations. Leadership spread throughout a network of people is more likely to flourish when certain "conditions" support it, including:

- *open flows of information*

- *flexible hierarchies*

- *distributed resources*

- *distributed decision-making*

- *loosening of centralized controls*

While some organizations have been courageously attempting to shift toward these types of conditions, our observation is that organizations like Clarke, who thrive in this shift, are embodying a cultural ingredient often invisible to the organizational charts, processes, structures, and practices that the rest of us can see. This ingredient is the experience of wholeness.

Wholeness happens when we invite either the entire organization/team/community into the room, or get the "whole story" into the room, by ensuring representation of every possible voice is included in the process.

Through our work with Appreciative Inquiry, the experience of wholeness has consistently turned tension into positive excitement, skepticism into collaboration, and indifference into inspired collective action. When we ask clients what happens when the whole system is in the room, the answers often include:

- It evokes trust. When everyone is there you don't have to feel suspicious about what the others will do – there are no others.

- It lets people see and experience a purpose greater than their own or their department's.

- You get the sense that you are connected to a goodness that comes from the power of the whole. You realize you really need one another.

- It satisfies the human need to be part of a larger community. It taps into our tribal consciousness. You feel like you belong

- It establishes credibility in the outcomes. When everyone is part of the decision you know it will stick. Public commitments engender responsibility.

- New norms form quickly. You start to value relationships and getting the "whole story."[3]

- People transcend the " I" and become a "We." What's common becomes apparent.

- It eliminates false assumptions about other people and other groups. When you get to know someone you realize they aren't exactly what you imagined them to be. You develop compassion for different people instead of judgements.

So, how do we practically design for the "experience of wholeness" to happen when we really want to unlock collective capability in any team of any size or type? From physics to psychology to research on high performing teams, there are some simple but powerful clues.

Our Answer to Google's 'Project Aristotle' Findings: Connection & Inclusion

In 2012, Google embarked on a research project, code named "Project Aristotle", to find out what leads to a high performing team. After extensive

---

[3]   pg. 2, *The Appreciative Inquiry Summit: An Emerging Methodology for Whole System Positive Change*, Diana Whitney, Ph.D., David L. Cooperrider, Ph.D.

research, the conclusion they arrived at was that high performing teams created an atmosphere of "psychological safety." Psychological safety, as Harvard Professor Amy Edmonson wrote in 1999, describes "a team climate characterized by interpersonal trust and mutual respect in which people are comfortable being themselves."

What we've learned at FLI is that we can actually choreograph group conversations, or what we call "conversational structure design," so that psychological safety is accelerated. How do we do this? The answer is shockingly simple, but takes a little planning to execute on. Through every conversation we facilitate, we maintain a conscious awareness of how we are inviting "connection and inclusion" from one conversation to the next.

To start, we make sure that as groups work through life-giving conversations, that we start with pairs or small groups, before we slowly move into medium sized or larger group conversations. Second, we ensure we are diversifying and mixing who is connecting with whom, in order to enable inclusion. Inclusion is often avoided for natural but unfortunate reasons - we stick with people like us (or who we like), we silo ourselves in our department, or even worse, it may be "us against them", even though we are on the same team.

Connection and inclusion honors the inherent desire for any group to experience the power of wholeness. Our belief is that every person walks into a room, group, or organization and wonders the same thing—can I be myself and still fit in here? What we've found is that designing group conversations to honor as many diverse connections as possible can accelerate this feeling of belonging. David Boehm, physicist and philosopher, reminds us that the root of the word "whole" means "healthy." When we facilitate connection and inclusion, we break down silos, we enable strengths to touch strengths, and we unlock new combinations of capabilities.

Remember that in practice, wholeness starts with ensuring that we bring as many voices as possible into our life-giving conversations. But wholeness, and the experience of connection and inclusion, often isn't experienced until we help these diverse voices to see and hear each other—eye to eye, heart to heart.

Time for an Evolutionary Leap

At each stage of human evolution—from the agrarian age to the industrial age to the information age, there have been radical changes in technology, power structures, belief systems, and how we organize and collaborate in groups. The collective disengagement and lack of meaning in the workplace, and eroding faith in our institutions (education, healthcare, and the government just to name a few) represent a possibility that we are due for another evolutionary leap.

I believe the collective pain that we feel is actually positive. It's a signal that something new is seeking to be born. For those looking to lead and manage into the future, we are called to courageously leap away from knowing, away from commanding and controlling, and away from separating work and humanity.

It's an evolutionary leap toward opening our minds by embracing inquiry, opening our hearts by seeing through the eyes of each other, and ultimately opening to the possibility that we can participate in shaping the future we most want. We can be at our collective best, when we connect and include the unique gifts and strengths of more and more voices.

Download the bonus worksheet 'Applying the Principles' at
juliereisler.com/masteryourself

BONUS APPENDIX

Bonus 1

Life Is A Classroom: How to Keep Learning

The best way to keep learning is to make a daily practice and habit of committing to your personal development. Whether it's reading *The Miracle Morning* and carving out time for the six highly effective practices, or even just choosing one to two habits that you do consistently, the importance is that you continue to study and grow yourself. I've coined the term becoming your "you-est you®" to indicate an ongoing exploration full of curiosity, growth, open-mindedness and appreciative-based questions to ask yourself each day. In this way, you will continue to become your "you-est you®" and crush it in all areas of life.

Use this worksheet to stay accountable and committed to keeping up your studies on yourself.

Date: _____

MORNING ROUTINE

SILENCE	AFFIRMATIONS	VISUALIZE	EXERCISE	READING	SCRIBING

How did you feel?

_____

_____

_____

Evening Check-in

List five things you're grateful for:

1. _____

2. _____

3. _____

4. _____

5. _____

One win to celebrate at work: _____

_____

_____

Bonus 2

Your Personalized Energy Assessment

Are you living in an energy emergency? Check all that apply to you. If you have 2 or more checked items in any category, you could be in an energy emergency! Take this assessment to find out:

Physical:

__ I often eat processed foods high in fat and sugar.

__ I rarely get seven to eight hours of sleep, and typically I don't feel well-rested.

__ I don't get much movement or any kind of exercise (less than two times/week).

__ I drink more than one cup of caffeinated drinks/day.

__ I don't drink 60+ oz of water a day.

__ I often skip breakfast or eat late at night.

Mindset:

__ I feel like life is passing me by, and I'm not as present as I'd like to be.

__ I often feel frustrated, negative, overwhelmed or stressed at work, and often at home as well.

__ There never seems to be enough time to finish all I need to do at work and for myself.

__ I am often overly engaged in and distracted by social media, TV, and games.

__ I don't remember the last time I paused to appreciate my surroundings or to reflect.

__ I often work late at night, on weekends and without breaks.

Emotional State:

__ I have difficulty expressing my emotions and often feel trapped and frustrated by them.

__ I am not always in tune with my emotional state and have a hard time assessing other's emotions.

__ I often become reactive to negative events, issues at work and other stresses rather than taking time to pause, reflect and be proactive with my response.

__ I often take my frustration or difficulties from work into my home life and have a hard time letting things go.

__ I don't make time for personal development or further developing my best self.

__ I am not utilizing my greatest strengths and skills in my work.

Bonus 3

Your Personalized Body Nourishment Assessment

Learn to tap into your own innate body wisdom and keep track of what foods work and don't work for your optimum performance. Use this assessment to raise your body wisdom awareness.

Examples of how you might feel: *energized, lethargic, sleepy, full, bloated, uncomfortable, joyful, eager, itchy, swollen, achy, invigorated, light.*

When I eat fruit, my body feels:

_____

_____

_____

_____

Specific fruits that I like are:

_____

_____

_____

_____

Specific fruits I don't like are:

_____

_____

_____

When I eat dairy, my body feels:

Dairy items I like are:

Dairy items I don't like are:

When I eat vegetables, my body feels:

_____

_____

_____

_____

Vegetables I like are:

_____

_____

_____

Vegetables I don't dig:

_____

_____

_____

How do I feel when I eat raw vs. cooked food?

_____

_____

When I eat meat, my body feels:

When I eat carbohydrates, my body feels:

When I eat packaged junk foods, I feel:

When I eat whole grains, I feel:

_____

_____

_____

_____

When I eat sugar, my body feels:

_____

_____

_____

_____

When I drink alcohol my body feels:

_____

_____

_____

_____

When I drink coffee my body feels:

_____

_____

_____

When I eat _____ my body feels:

When I eat _____ my body feels:

When I eat _____ my body feels:

When I drink _____ my body feels:

_____

_____

_____

_____

Remember to pause and reflect after you eat or drink. What are you becoming aware of? Touch base again twenty minutes later; how do you feel now? What are you noticing? Any patterns? Jot them down below.

_____

_____

_____

_____

_____

Could you try asking yourself how you feel after you eat anything for the next week?

If you need extra support, bring on an accountability partner, friend or confidant who can help support you in your goals to better nourish your body.

Bonus 4

Your Workplace Wholeness Wheel

Rate where you are right now for each category. Notice where you are on the workplace wholeness wheel and where you'd like to be. Use this wheel monthly, quarterly, or as often as you'd like as a way to visually check in with how you are designing and living your life. **Note: 1 = low, 10 = high**

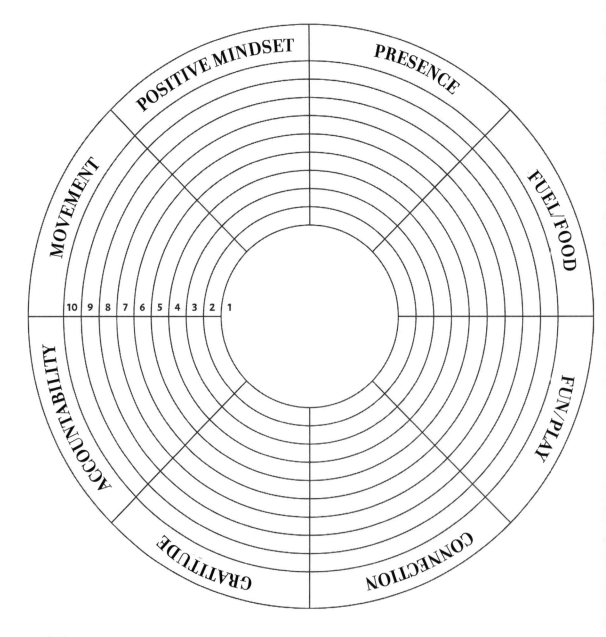

Bonus 5

Guided Breathing Meditation for Stress Release

1. Find a comfy place to sit or, if you want, you can even lie down (watch out for dozing off). I recommend setting a timer that you can see and starting small with three minutes, working your way to five and eventually ten minutes. However, any amount of time sitting still and breathing is worthwhile.

2. Ground your feet (or bottom) to the floor. I like to imagine roots coming out of my feet, as though I'm a tree, and spreading throughout the ground, reaching wide and far and getting deeper and more connected.

3. Sitting comfortably, with shoulders down and chest relaxed, start to notice your breath. A trick I like to use is putting one hand on my chest (you can think of sending good feelings to your heart) and the other on my stomach. You'll want your hand on your stomach—not the one on your heart—to move in and out. Most of us breathe from our chests until we re-train ourselves to breathe from our diaphragm and belly.

4. Sitting with calm and ease, begin by inhaling for two breaths and exhaling for two breaths. When you inhale, you'll want your stomach to fill with air like a big balloon. On the exhale, let out your breath and imagine the balloon deflating. Your belly will get full of air on the inhale and deflate with your exhale.

5. If you'd like, breathe in for two counts, hold for two counts, and let it out for two counts. This is called a 2:2:2 ratio and is easy to pick up.

6. Once you get still and in the flow of your breath, you could choose a word that fills you with calm, such as "peace" or "flow." Important note: your mind will still have thoughts and feel like it's jumping all over the place. This is normal. You are human, after all. Do not worry about this. I'd invite you to think about your thoughts like clouds passing

through the sky. They eventually pass, and you can just go right back to your 2:2:2 ratio.

7. Allow yourself to feel what it would be like if your whole body were filled with the word you chose. Breathe this word in and out through your nose. As you exhale, let go of any negative thoughts like stress, worry, or concern.

8. Before ending your meditation, focus on an area of life for which you are extremely grateful. Allow that feeling of appreciation to fill your body.

9. As you end your meditation, end with repeating your word to yourself.

10. Enjoy the benefits of creating calmer and more peaceful while allowing your body to rest, recharge, and reboot. Feel free to add to this practice in any way you see fit. For a free download of this guided meditation by yours truly, go here: juliereisler.com/stressreleasemeditation

Bonus 6: PhD in YOU in Business Resources

Books:

The Miracle Morning, Hal Elrod

The Soul of Success, Jack Canfield

Good to Great, Jim Collins

You Must Write a Book, Honorée Corder

Lean In, Sheryl Sandberg

The War of Art, Steven Pressfield

Willpower Doesn't Work, Benjamin Hardy

Drive, Daniel H. Pink

The 7 Habits of Highly Effective People, Stephen Covey

Conversations Worth Having, Jaqueline Stavros

The Art of Possibility, Rosamund Stone Zander & Benjamin Zander

The One Thing, Gary Keller and Jay Papasan

Expert Secrets, Russell Brunson

Buddha's Brain, Rick Hanson

Think and Grow Rich, Napoleon Hill

Get a PhD in YOU, Julie Reisler

YouTube:

"Start with Why," Simon Sinek

"The Power of Vulnerability," Brené Brown

"The Happiness Advantage," Shawn Achor

"Your Body Language May Shape Who You Are," Amy Cuddy

"Hardwiring Happiness," Dr. Rick Hanson

"Why We Do What We Do," Tony Robbins

"My Stroke of Insight," Jill Bolte Taylor

"Could One Question Uplift and Unite Humanity," Jon Berghoff

"How to Speak So That People Want to Listen," Julian Treasure

"Everyday Leadership," Drew Dudley

"Microbiome: Gut Bugs and You," Warren Peters

"Words Get in The Way," Julie Reisler

"Get a PhD in YOU," Julie Reisler

Further Support to Crush It:

Calling all change makers and self-starters! If you're interested in further support and accountability with your career, business or even starting a side hustle, I would love to have you in my Monetize Your Purpose coaching program! Find out more at **juliereisler.com/purpose**.

GRATITUDE

To my husband, Heath, for always believing in me and supporting
my dreams to uplift the world. You uplift me.

To my children, who have my heart and are my daily teachers.

To my magical mentor, coach and dear friend, Honorée Corder, without
whom I would not have the wisdom in writing this book.

To Jon Berghoff, teacher, coach and friend; Maureen (Mo) McKenna, wise
mentor and friend; Dr. Jacqueline Stavros, author of the bestselling book,
Conversations Worth Having, and also wise mentor and friend; Zoe Galvez
and Betsy Crouch, co-founders of ImprovHQ and dear friends; all of my colleagues and friends in the LEAF (Leading Experiential Appreciative Facilitation)
and FLI (Flourishing Leadership Institute) community; Gib Mason and Marc
Kolp at UMBC Training Centers for extraordinary leadership, guidance and
encouragement in my endeavors; my fellow entrepreneurial peers; and dear
friends from the Quantum Leap Mastermind community with and including
Hal Elrod and Jon Berghoff.

I cherish and thank each of you for your ongoing
encouragement, support, and vision.

WHO IS JULIE

Julie is a Doctor of Potentiality. Author and Life Designer® Julie Reisler is the founder and CEO of Empowered Living, a Life Design and personal development company. Julie is a multi-time TEDx speaker, host of *The You-est You*® podcast and meditation teacher on the popular app, Insight Timer. Julie has a master's degree in health & wellness coaching, with a concentration in nutrition, and more than twelve certifications in leadership, health and well-being. Julie runs a coaching program, *Monetize Your Purpose*, for change makers, entrepreneurs and coaches. Julie is the author of *Get a PhD in YOU*, the companion journal to this book, and creator of the documentary and course, *Hungry for More*. Julie is also on the faculty at Georgetown University in their coaching program and is a Lululemon Ambassador. Julie is passionate about helping you to master your inner world so you can crush it at work and beyond. To learn more about Julie, go to juliereisler.com.

Podcast: The You-est You®
Website: http://www.JulieReisler.com
IG: @JulieReisler
Facebook: @JulieReislerLifeDesigner
LinkedIn: @JulieReisler

BOOK JULIE TO SPEAK

"To say that Julie is an amazing speaker or teacher does not do her justice. She is a powerful Thought Leader who has the ability to bring a group of anyone, including Combat Veterans, to a place of pure serenity. As a keynote speaker at our Summit and TEDx LadyBirdLake, she had the audience completely mesmerized. At her breakout teaching session, I witnessed Veterans who had never talked about their experiences, openly share with the group their struggles as well as their proudest moments, seamlessly and without reserve. Women and men, young and old....she enables people to be the very best version of themselves! The greatest gift I can think of is to give someone the gift of Julie teaching."

- Cassaundra Melgar-C'De Baca, Executive Producer for TEDx Lady Bird Lake and CEO of VETTED.

Julie Reisler is a leading Life Design expert. She is a multi-time TEDx and motivational speaker, podcast host and international facilitator and coach who will bring energy, wit, wisdom, and expertise to your audience. Julie has inspired and guided professionals to master their inner world to master their outer world. Her genuine charm and expert knowledge are guaranteed to help your audience, business, or group achieve the success they desire, all while interacting along the way. Book Julie as your Keynote Speaker and you're guaranteed to make your event and program highly energizing and valuable!

FOR MORE INFORMATION VISIT:
JULIEREISLER.COM/SPEAKING

Made in the USA
Middletown, DE
02 May 2019